Macramé for Beginners

Complete guide for beginners, it will guide you step by step in improving the art of macrame, inside will be included models and handmade projects for the home and garden

Celandine Kyrie

Table of Contents

Introduction

Discover all you need to know to make custom macramé projects. Go beyond novice to knowledgeable artisan in a short period of time with our macramé for beginners' guide, our macramé supplies list, and our individual macramé recommend-dations.

This book is here to take all of the suspense out of this thrilling, cool yet traditional mastering trend known as macramé. You just need to realize that you can do this. However, you may always have your skepticism, so worry not - this book is here for you. It is going to satisfy all your concerns and potentially wipe away any remaining hesitations and questions. By the time you are done reading this book, you'll a) have a lovely, inexpensive DIY macramé art for both your indoors and garden area and b) be willing to apply macramé to your list of skills.

Macramé is a form of knotting and tangling cords to make beautifully stunning items for your house, namely wall hangings, plant hangers, and jewelry. The success of DIY macramé has not decreased much over the past couple of years, making it such a perfect hobby for anyone to pick up. Through this book, you will be able to learn various knots and methods, which are used for macramé. You can progress by working up your base as you move through every chapter, or literally dip in and out if you want. Through systematic directions, each method is clearly outlined and demonstrated through photos and illustrations, making it simple for rookies.

At the conclusion of the book, there are fabulous tasks, outlined in systematic detail with 'you'll need' specifications, and there are even a few mini macramé project ideas included so you can learn a method and do it right away. Although the examples of the methodology were operated with regular cords for clear accountability, the project ideas illustrate how the simplicity of maximum clarity can be improved by picking various cords or strings, thicker or thinner, based on how you want to use the material. You will even find out how incorporating beads will boost the methods for yet more spectacular outcomes.

Chapter 1:
Basics of the Art of Macramé

Aknot is a fundamental process of bringing two loose ends together and locking them. We never pay a second glance to the play, but there is so much more to a knot. From the earliest civilizations, Knots have been the daily routine of humankind who used it in a functional application and even made it into divine, scientific, mystical, medical, creative and decorative artifacts. Macramé is one case where men turned the basic act of knot tying into an artistic medium.

The fragility of cloth objects is a daunting challenge faced by archaeologists-they disintegrate well before we can discover them to examine and document. This was the same issue with finding the macramé's roots. Experts confidently believe that knotting originated for humankind because of the need for building and work formed by man. The oldest actual samples of knots discovered were dated between 15,000 and 17,000 BC, although they believe that knotting maybe 250,000 years ago and 2,500,000 years old predates the utilizing explosion.

1.1 What is Macramé?

Knotting and weaving are techniques that have been utilized for decades, and in recent times, there has been increasing curiosity about how they can be utilized about art applications. While very distinct, knots and ringlets are closely intertwined in several ways: they involve ropes or strings as a foundation, they are designed with basic movements that can be merged to build very complicated constructs, and they can gain from jewelry embellishments.

Macramé is a decorative tangling technique and design. Sewing strings or cords into one basic or complicated loop, without hooks, accomplish it by hand. A braided rope and a few simple knots are all required for an enthusiast to discover the opportunities of creating jewelry, clothes, wall art, or flower holds. Thousands of years of the Chinese form of Macramé followed the American trend for the art in the early 1990s. Western Macramé also draws fiber-artists, sewers, and artisans.

Modern Macramé requires several various paints or textured strings. You may pick cotton, silk, linen, embroidery floss, rope, base metal thread, hemp, or even kite rope from the infinite sorts of twine. The spinning, color, rigidity, and length would all influence the polished Macramé appearance. You may also attach extensions to thematize your job inside the fastened design. To feature or highlight their items, many artisans acquire sea items like seashells, pearls or beads, charms, or tassels constructed of clay, glass, steel, or plastic.

In some main ways, the Chinese Macramé varies from the western Macramé. Next, there is just one section of string divided in half, such that at the bottom two strings join the tie and two leaves. The bits, too, are often rectangular and double-sided, leaving a pocket in the middle. Within the tangled folds, men locked semi-precious minerals, sculptures, or even flowers. Two titles of decorative ties are the Fist of Man, the Double Coin, and Good Luck.

As with many handicrafts, Macramé initiated with practical use. The first Macramé was done in hand-woven rugs to bind off the edges of strings so that they would not unravel. Macramé was often used to create and repair fishing vessels, and anglers used the loops used to bind boats, ships, and cannons to create jewelry and textile materials. Macramé was used over the century to manufacture a range of useful and artistic pieces like wall hangings, shoes, fabrics, even bedspreads. The same ties are often used for creating lanyards and necklaces in a common kids' art utilizing vinyl "gimp."

1.2 The Origin of Macramé

Macramé is a French term that refers to knot; it is one of the earliest art styles. The early Persians and Assyrians (2300 B.C.) fined this craft with considerable ability. Afterward, the Arabs took the art style to Europe, and the Europeans to America, where the communities of the Caribbean used it to create their traditional hammocks knotted in. Yes, hand-knotted chandeliers, plant hangers & gadgets lined every nook and cranny in the seventies and are making a tremendous comeback now, but this art has been handed Bottom from all across the world for over thousands of years. Let us discover the modern Macramé origins.

The significance of Macramé during the 13th century is primarily related to Arabic weavers, who utilized ornamental knots to wrap up the loose ends of hand-woven fabrics. Even so, decorative knot tying on ritualistic textiles along with wall hangings can also be dated directly to China in the third century. While it may be difficult to identify the very first Macramé ever created, kudos to those Arab Artisans of the thirteenth century, the art incrementally introduced to Europe and ultimately became a popular theme for sailors. Knots had numerous useful applications on their ships, but during extended trips, the elegant knot tying held the hands and minds occupied. In addition, they would advertise and trade their braided goods like hammocks, straps, and hats at the harbor. Macramé Knot-tying continued to be a major hobby and reason to adorn clothes and textiles throughout the Victorian era when it primarily went out of fashion until its wild and glamorous reversion in the 1970s.

In the mid-1800s, after "Sailors' Aid" societies built libraries on vessels in an attempt to teach and educate rowdy shipmates, Knot-tying dropped out of fashion as a sport. As per the Ashley Book of Knots (1944), which many fanatics regard to be the "knot bible" with over 3,000 layouts, published by Clifford Warren Ashley, "The reality that a sailor could not read and at the same period use his hands could be acknowledged as largely responsible. It was unavoidable that when the sailor began to read, he would overlook the art" Then sailors suddenly took up imaginative knotting again in the "second quarter of the 20th century," but Ashley refuses to examine precisely why. "The hand-eye of the sailor, long bondsmen to publications and novels, were again available," a book author wrote. Sailors generated their woman peers' belts and handbags while listening to seemingly outstanding information technology, the radio.

Nevertheless, fancy ropework and adornment stayed niche essentially — until the 1970s, when every layout magazine and bohemian composer seemed to hang a macramé plant strap in the corner. (Macramé is just one artisan-style, mostly represented by square knots.) In addition to tassels and placemats, people were DIYing photo frames, travel bags, hammocks, swimsuits, wall hangings, and so much more. In a 1973 research in the New York Times titled "The Art of Knot-Tying Revived," publisher and knot professional John Hensel claimed, "It appears that rope work isn't only being consumed by elderly people or children, but also by younger people." He addressed that knotwork is an affordable art; if you cannot access a twine length, just sew a blind cord in the Veneto.

The macramé phenomenon had been so widespread it hung on humorous by the late 1970s. One speculative hipster even generated a macramé Christmas tree that the New York Times could not help but document the monstrosity. Replicas cost around $2,500. Yet a devoted fandom of weavers continued on as mainstream knotting gained momentum from the news. The volume of knot literature was growing, and internet creation was democratizing what was once a trendier medium of art. Design and DIY creators released videos, and are still popular today with their bohemian wall hangings. Such designs, however, also almost took the place of cliché — if not for the latest craze to restore the limelight in fashion. From another inflated trend research, this time in the Washington

Post, millennials cannot afford a house with gardens to help relieve their existential insecurity, so they line studios with thousands of flowers in one-bedroom apartments. Some also put Bottom Sunday brunch arrangements (avocado toast, ergo), choosing misting and fertilizing for hours.

Basic macramé has a range of different knots, with the most excellently-known being the square knot and the half knot, which, when mixed, make borders (overlaid or woven) or braids to ornament bags or fabrics, potted plants, tables, wall art, and fabrics.

Macramé Vocabulary to Get Familiar With

Before you practically start working on your first macramé project, pause for a moment or two to become comfortable with the knotting or macramé terms that are regularly used in step instructions, several of which are summarized here.

- **Working end:** It is the end of the cord used to tie the knot.
- **Starting end:** The contrary end to the working end-both ends is working ends if you start in the midpoint of a cord.
- **Crosspoint:** Where one chord overlaps the other, an overhand cross point is when the end of the work is at the top and an underhand cross point when the end of the work is underneath.
- **U-shaped bend:** Also identified as a bright, it is often done via the knot as a direction to knit a cord.

- **Circled:** The cord moves one or two knotted threads through it.
- **Coiled:** Multiple times the cord will roll around one or more layers.
- **Loop in a clockwise direction:** Also known as an overhand loop, which is where the end of the working chord moves in a clockwise direction and over itself again.
- **Loop in an anti-clockwise direction (clockwise):** Occasionally made reference to as an underhand loop, it is where the end of the work goes around in an anti-clockwise direction and again over itself.
- **Weave:** This refers to going in a knot with a U-shaped bend or working end and under subsequent cords.
- **Firm up:** Firm up the knot until the cords are stable, although not stiff enough to alter the knot itself.
- **Core cord:** Within other cords and threads, this is a static cord. The central cords can become working cords in macramé, or even the other way round.
- **Base Cord:** This cord also shapes a necklace's basic shape or can be replaced by a finding, for example, a strong loop, strapping, or chain. Typically, the operating cords are connected to the base cord with the head-knots of the lark.

Tatting and Macramé

Although all crafts involve knotting and stitching, Tatting is distinctly different from Macramé, as it is solely artistic. It was primarily designed to emulate point lace, which was common during the late nineteenth century when garments and window curtains were mostly adorned with edgings of lace.

Whereas, looking at the other side, Macramé is more utilitarian than artistic, even if certain people utilized knotting in painted hoops, canes, tables, lamps, or even knife grips. Macramé focuses on making a stand-alone item out of cords. Beading and other materials, such as tubes, can be used to improve the finished product's look.

The technique used to create the piece is also another distinction between Macramé and Tatting. Tatting needles and shuttles are used to direct the design across the loops. Macramé requires no instrument to construct the knots; it needs only agile fingertips and a vivid imagination. Eventually, Tatting requires the use of very thin threads to build their designs of lacy. Macramé uses cords bigger than these do. In addition, if the cords are 1 mm in diameter, they will always be too wide to use in Tatting.

Tatting is a classic type of lacework. If you are a fan of crocheting, weaving, engraving, and Macramé, it means you will also have a fair opportunity to try Tatting. If you especially like crochet thread, you will consider tatting fun. Tatting is utilized to make lace edgings and ornamental napkins that are pretty much like those used in crochet.

So what exactly is Tatting?

Tatting is a process of making elaborate knotwork utilizing threads and materials. It is a counterpart to many other techniques and incorporates the various methods used in them all. You render loops, for instance, in addition to which you also rely on weaving to produce the shape of tatting silk. Culturally Tatting has been used mainly for incorporating thorough edging and decoration to improve the appeal of the garments.

Forms of Tatting

In addition, there are many specific styles of Tatting. The specific styles can depend on the resources you are utilizing. Begin to dive into the technique, and uncover:

- Cro-tatting: This form is a blend of Tatting and crochet. This technique uses the primary device, a tiny crochet needle. The ties that you make come from Tatting, though. If you are a knitter who wishes to grasp the concept of Tatting, then that is a perfect starting point.

- Shuttle tatting: The initial design of the craft was possibly in this shape. Tatting from the knotwork that merchants did was handed on. They used a Weaving shuttle-like tool, but smaller in scale and diameter.

- Needle tatting: This style uses a needle rather than a shuttle, as its title implies. Many individuals see this as being the simpler of the two, especially if you are an artist who has accustomed to the cast-on that is comparable to how you begin a needle tatting work.

Origin of Tatting

Tatting actually developed centuries ago in some way, when anglers and hunters experimented with various knots to build their vessels and nets. In the nineteenth century, it really emerged into its own as art. Throughout numerous ways, the art has common names: frivolity throughout Europe, knotting in England, and Tatting in America.

Tatting was common in Ireland in the times of the potato famine, as was crochet. People in Ireland desperately struggled to get by. They would make delicate laces utilizing yarn, shuttle, pin, or hook only. In an attempt to help their relatives, they will market such laces to wealthy men, mostly to England.

Tatting was common in America during the 1930s, 1940s, and 1950s, as were other types of needlework. In order to make tatted doilies, women would use tatting techniques to create common lace collars. Whether you are searching for women's antique publications from those times, you will find designs and tutorials for Tatting.

Tatting Stitches

Once you begin Tatting for the first time, you will sound like you have had to muster up an entire foreign vocabulary. Always note when you continue knitting or crocheting, it is the same approach. You will be fast to get the hold of it. It is likely that you have always been confused by "yarn over, pull through," or acronyms like "hdc" before you began crocheting, however after you have mastered the art, reading those directions will become simple. Like all those other handicrafts, Tatting has its own central stitches you can discover when you start. Essentially, to get going, what you would need to learn is that Tatting requires a number of strings, loops, stitches, and rings. You make loops, creatively merge them to get patterns, and use variation to construct different types of unique details.

The most popular stitch in Tatting is labeled the dual stitch, which is a knot with a half hook. When you make a loop as you do a double stitch, it creates a picot. Typically, as you combine motifs, you do enter via a picot. Any other specific terms that you can see as you operate on a tatting design include:

- Chain (Basically a double-stitched series)
- Ring (which is a combination of double stitches shaped to create a shape like a circle or an oval)
- Center Ring
- Separate (the sum of distance in picots you would be leaving)

Uses of Tatting

Historically, Tatting has been used for edgings and applying vintage-inspired lace edging to every home furnishings project, or dress is perfect art. Nevertheless, Tatting may also be used to build a good collection of fashionable lace designs. Of starters, Tatting is good to create delicate string jewelry.

Tatting fits well when it comes to luxurious designs as well. For, e.g., if you would like to design your own wedding face covering for that venture, then Tatting is a wonderful art. It is also a great option for other precious things like infant booties and Holiday decorations when you choose to do it a bit special, utilizing Tatting before you send them to produce a customized lace border on the flashcards.

To put it another way, any task that looks good with a bit of lace embellished to it is a task that would be an amazing way to attempt Tatting.

1.3 Supplies Needed to Create a Macramé

In case you are already a skilled beader or artisan, a lot of the tools and much of the mentioned items are stuff you would find in your workbox anyway. You should not need to buy anything at once because you can still modify, but utilizing a particular item or the machines and equipment mentioned is safer for optimal performance. Methods of knotting and sewing can be used in a massive range of distinct yarn and cords. In this portion of the chapter, the options available are examined.

Cord selection

Conduct tests with various materials after you have mastered a methodology, and you would be shocked at the results. When dealing with a gentle cord such as satin rattail or embroidery cotton, knots can lack form, and the outline can be even clearer by utilizing a stiffer cord such as SuperlonTM, wax cotton, or round leather thong. Take into account how you want the final item to look, and select your cord or thread appropriately before you begin. Recall that every one of these cords is accessible in a variety of densities and can be employed either individually or in several packages.

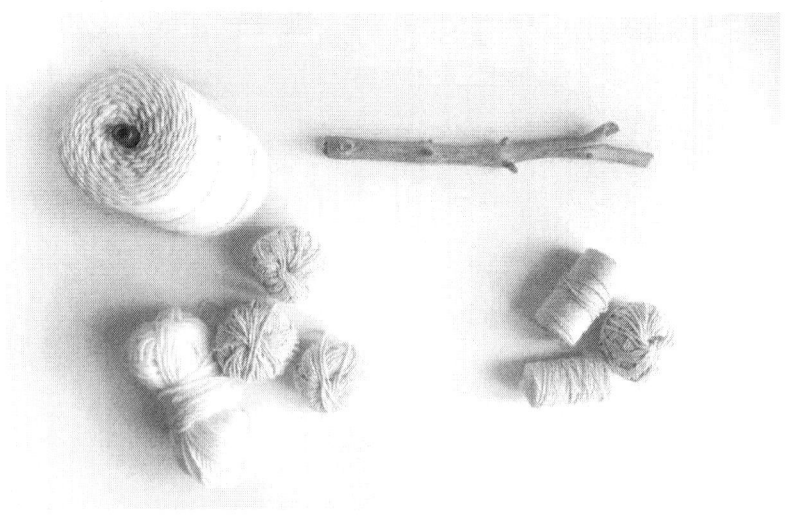

- **Cord satin (rattail)** - A silky cord has a high shine and is comes in a multitude of densities: the bug tail is 1 mm thick, the mouse-tail is 1.5 mm thick, and the rattail is 2 mm thick, but in practice, everything is now called rattail. The cord is relatively lightweight, but it does not very easily help the form of the ties, and it is not hardwearing.

- **Linen Cord** - Linen cording comes with an advanced range of colors and concentrations that make it highly suitable for many styles of draping. Linen has the versatility and variety that so many other cording styles do not possess, which makes it ideal for Macramé designs that need to be solid and sturdy. Linen cording is mostly used in wall art in Macramé and looks fantastic when paired with other cording styles, such as silk or cotton. However, the one aspect you need to note is that linen cording can unravel quickly, and you will have to make sure to finish the tasks thoughtfully.

- **Wax cord made from cotton** - Wax cotton cord matches a variety of techniques. Watch out for a thicker 3 mm belt, which fits particularly well for independent knots and tangled braids because it keeps its form good. Narrower wax cotton is suitable for macramé, and beads are easy to string. These are sold in natural colors and a variety of colors, often reflecting recent trends in design.

- **Chinese Cord Knotting** - This braided nylon cord preserves its circular form while it is running. The denser cords are generally available in 0.4–3 mm and are especially suited for fastening techniques. Finer cords are common for bead bracelets made from macramé and Shamballa style. Search for the largest color options online, although you will note the color selections for the denser cords are not as broad.

- **Leather thong** - Round leather thong, because it is a strong belt, allows a nice distinct tie. It comes in a variety of densities from around 0.5 mm up to 6 mm. The lighter cords are ideal for linking knots, and the heavier cords are best fit for use as a framework for winding the knots together. Leather thong comes in natural colors with a broad range of hues. Pearlescent finishes are especially appealing, typically in light pastels, as are the various densities of the snakeskin impact cords.

- **Hemp -** With Macramé jewelry designs, Hemp is favored over other fiber strings. This is because it quickly ties, so it can keep the ties well. Hemp is soft enough to carry on your skin easily, and it is perfect for all jewelry designs. While the jute cord is somewhat close to hemp cording, it is much too messy to be used for projects in Macramé jewelry. Hemp comes in varied finishes and sizes. It covers Hemp by thread weight all the way through extreme roping of Hemp. Hemp has a natural medium tan color, but you can purchase jewelry weight hemp, which is colored in a variety of colors.

- **Faux suede -** This plain microfiber cord looks like natural leather suede, but is far more pliable than the actual thing and offers knots or knotted braids a very different feel. =It is usually 3 mm long and in a variety of colors.

- **Embroidery threads -** Stranded petrel cotton and cotton are just two widely accessible threads that can be used to knot, plait and braid. Embroidery threads are gentle and will not hold a knot's shape firmly, but when integrated with stiffer cords, they look great. The range of hues and colors is much broader than for other cords so exciting color schemes are possible. While embroidery strings are normally matte, a bit of sparkle can be applied with platinum embroidery threads.

- **SuperlonTM -** SuperlonTM (often shortened to S-Lon) is a nylon twisted high strength cord that was initially used for

19

furniture. It is available in widths of 0.5 mm, and 0.9 mm, and both are acceptable for micro macramé and other knotting methodologies where a fine braid or finish is required. These cords are great for adding beads to your fastening or weaving and can be blended with denser cords for a texture change. Both sizes come in a variety of neutrals and contemporary different shades.

- **Paracord** - This chunky cord usually comes in two densities: paracord 550 (4 mm) has seven strands Bottom the center, and paracord 450 (2 mm) has four center strands. Paracord is ideal for making bracelets and other ornaments from single knots and single-width knotted braid, and because it is quite heavy, it is prevalent for men's jewelry. The cord is accessible in a multitude of bright and dark solid colors and in many multicolored patterns.

Calculate How Much Cording You Need to Use

You will have to determine how long your cording will last. While most initiatives would offer you the required dimensions, you must have some experience in how this calculation is done. Even so, the ends of the cording should be three 1/2 to 4 times longer than the bit you plan to create since the cording is divided in half for knotting it is sized 7 to 8 times longer than the required amount. For instance: if the Macramé design has a finished size of 1 yard, you will like to calculate the cording from one end to the other 7 to 8 yards. Therefore, as each end of the knotting is repeated, there would be two ends, with each end being three 1/2 to 4 yards high. Make sure you carefully weigh the ends, as you would not want to run out of cording and have to attach to the frame. Getting extra cording is much better than going out and putting in an awkward spot in the build.

You would definitely want to create free sample Macramé designs, so you can estimate how the cording knots are calculated and how long they are made. Solid cording can take up more time in fastening than lighter ones, and when determining how much cording to use, you may need to account for this. Create a sampler measuring around 3 inches by 6 inches so you can gauge the duration of the cord and see how many ends the design would require for the distance. Determining the number of ends: bind four ends into a Square Knot and calculate the width of the knot. If the knot diameter is 1/2 inch, you will realize that for your project template, you need eight ends to the inch. When you decide what Macramé layout, you want to get you to work with the ties, and you decide just how the cording is going to tie and how you can gauge the shape and how it feels.

Wire

The wire is not commonly used for stitching techniques since it is difficult to connect the wire without it being kinked, but certain knots produced Utilizing more of a wrapping method, for example, the pipa knot, may be employed in metal. Wire can be successfully used for any Kumihimo braid, particularly wraps of finer wire, and it is included in certain knotting and braiding finishing techniques. The wire used for fastening and weaving techniques has to withstand breaking even when it is repeatedly bent back and forth. Many craft wires have a core of copper, which makes them appropriate, but you may play with wire of all sorts. The key jewelry wires are evaluated here but understand that it is easier to control two or slimmer wires than one dense wire.

- **Copper wires** - Copper wire is appropriate for exploring both stitching and weaving techniques because it is a cheap material. Most craft wires have a core of copper with enameled colors and plated metal finishes. For copper design wires, you don't really get a preference of strength, but those are considered marketed exclusively for sewing or knitting to be smoother and less likely to snap. Recall, too, that lighter wires are simpler to treat than denser wires.
- **Wire made of aluminum** - Aluminum wire may be thicker than core copper wires since it is much gentler, but also use nylon-jaw plier wire to prevent damage to the wire.

- **Silver Wire** - Although pricey, the silver wire will raise any jewelry project to a different level. It is available in a variety of thicknesses, with the most popular being soft, semi-hard and firm, and also numerous cross-sections such as oval, rectangle, rectangular, and D-shaped. Choose a soft quality wire because work is simpler – you will note that only half-hard wire is difficult to operate.

- **Coated Wires** - It's worth playing with wrapped wires, whether paper, plastic or fine thread wrapped, because they're less susceptible to kink, and you're likely to get unexpected outcomes.

Beads

Beads may be added in a variety of ways to all knotting and braiding techniques, either during weaving or knotting or afterward. Beads come in all kinds of colors, finishes, shapes, and sizes, but the depth is paramount for fastening and weaving so the beads can easily be fastened onto the cord. When you go searching for charms, it is a smart idea to carry a piece of cord with you.

- **Seeds Beeds -** This is a common word used to define the minute glass beads predominantly used for bead sewing and stringing. Basic seed beads (rocailles) are doughnut-shaped, and the most popular sizes are 15 to 3 (1–5,5 mm) with 15 (1 mm) being the tiniest; cylinder-shaped beads, often known as delicas or magnificas, have wider holes, and the double delicacies may be strung onto 1 mm thread. Look for odd patterns such as triangle, hex, or charlotte beads or for various forms such as papillon (or peanut) beads and magatamas (drop beads), too.

- **Large Beads -** From plain wood beads to beautiful pearls and crystals, there are so many unique beads that could be used in braiding methods, and the selection is yours. The size of the bead hole does not actually need to limit you because certain beads have shockingly wide holes, like the Swarovski Mini-bead collection, where only the 6 mm beads fit into 1 mm thread. Beads in the Pandora model have very wide holes and can suit more than 6 mm thread.

- **Focal Beads -** These extremely broad beads are also used for a piece of jewelry as a focal point. Utilizing a bail, you can suspend pendant beads on braids, or attach cords to large ring beads for macramé work or other knotting techniques. Remember, too, that you can attach large beads between two braid lengths that have been completed with end caps.

Findings

Findings are all the small pieces, usually crafted of metal, used to create and finish jewelry objects or other items. Several of the findings are used to protect the raw edges of cords or braids, and the correct size and shape are important to choose from. Keep a large set of finds in your workbox so you can produce and complete various pieces.

- **Cord Ends** - Some types used for finishing single cords have lugs that you attach with pliers around the thread; others are tubular and are sealed either with adhesive or with an internal crimping loop. One of the ancient finding styles may be cylindrical or cone-shaped. Inside the coil of wire, tuck the cord or braid, then use pliers to pull just the end ring to safeguard it.

- **Spring ends** - These findings, cone-shaped or bell-shaped, can either have a hole at the top or end with a loop. Utilizing jeweler adhesive to protect the braid in all types for better performance.

- **End cones** - End caps either are conical, circular or rectangular variants of end cones, with a cavity at the top or a ring or circle ready-to-finish. Utilize jewelry adhesive to protect the braid in all types for better performance.

- **End caps** - These are constructed, as the title suggests, to protect the raw closure of the ribbon but can be used to complete flat braids or cords. Utilize nylon-jaw pliers to cover the ribbon crimp over the braid, to avoid injury.

- **Ribbon Crimps** - Fastening and weaving methods need nothing in the way of specialized hardware, and most - or artisans would certainly still have the supplies available in their workbox, and you will be able to start started right away.

Jewelry tools

To make braids or to knot into jewelry, a simple collection of three tools is required. Buying good-quality, fine tools is always worthwhile as these will help you finish things smoothly and professionally, but resist micro-tools as these will make your wrists numb when used for lengthy stretches.

- **Wire Cutters** - Spend a little extra on wire cutters because they help life a ton. Use side cutters, or ideally flush-cutters that cut wire or headpins to a straight end. Remember to cut towards the work or to face away from the tail with the flat side of the cutters. These pliers are used for making wire or headpin loops. The jaws are cone-shaped, so you can differ the loop size by working for small loops near the top of the jaws and for larger loops near the bottom. Still function the same exact distance, to create loops of the same duration.

- **Round Nose Pliers** - They are used to move wire and headpins or to open and shut the jumping loops. In addition, search for relatively smooth surfaces on the inside of the jaws – pinholes from the local hardware shop are unsuitable because apart from being too wide, they are likely to have deep grip serrations that will weaken the metal.

Specialized instruments

This kit can allow you to finish jewelry in a skilled way, but not necessary, so consider making the investment if you can.

- **Bent-Nose pliers** - These are effectively snipe-nose pliers with a right-angle bend in the jaws, which allows you to get into strange postures and hold wire or headpins at an easier position as needed.
- **Nylon-jaw pliers** - These pliers have a gentler material that covers the metal jaws in order to avoid injury to softer wires and results. They come as the round-nose or flat-nose pliers.
- **Crimp Pliers** - These pliers come in three sizes – micro, regular and macro – and are especially used to narrow crimps tidily around bead string wire. Adapt the pliers to wire density and crimp depth.
- **Split-ring pliers** - These will definitely help to prevent broken nails with a specially designed tip for opening split rings.
- **Awl** - An awl is useful for pushing cords and braids into metal findings and easing them.

- **Warp posts** - Clamp around the top of the surface of work and divide a certain gap for twisting long cord lengths.

Scissors

Maintain two or three various types of scissors specifically for thread and cord-cutting and do not use them for paper cutting, as this will deflect the blades very rapidly. Moderately sized scissors are optimal for length chopping of threads and cords, and slightly smaller scissors with pointed spots are ideal for smooth cutting of ends. Needles There are all kinds of needles that can make ending braids and knotting or thread beads easier.

Sewing needles

After wrapping a selection of different sizes of sewing needles allows you to sew through braids or safe finishes. Sharps have a tiny eye, but they are quite robust and can be used to sew small seed beads into stiffer strings. Embroidery needles have extended eyes to facilitate the threading.

- **Tapestry needles -** They have a comparatively blunt tip and wide eye and are handy to thread larger clusters onto a rope or to move knots into place.
- **Beading needles -** Fine beading needles can be utilized to attach to braids or to cover joins seed beads and other tiny beads. Optimal for size 11 seed beads and size 12 or 13 for size 15 seed beads, a size ten needle. Keep a decent

collection, as the better needles will bend and split in specific.

- **Twisted wire needles -** Clipping fine wire over the jaws of round-nose pliers and spinning the tails together can make your own needles. Conversely, they can be purchased in a variety of sizes to string beads onto a cord or thread, or to pull threads or cords to function or smoothen ends through ringlets.
- **Big eye needles -** Such long needles with two pointed tips are good for stringing beads on multi-strands of fine strings, but stop utilizing a small space to drawcords as the two fine rods that allow the needle break at the welded edge.

Pins

- **Dressmaker's pins -** Useful for tagging braids at a specific length, layout beads or adornments, or positioning wrapped threads.
- **Map pins -** Such small pins with ball ends are suitable to protect cords and strings as macramé functions. Plug it onto a corkboard or plastic core frame.

Adhesives

These are a number of various glues that can be used to attach cords and strings to create jewelry and other accessories. Choose the best adhesive to match the fabrics that you adhere to, and try to allow the glue to dry properly before use for 24 hours.

- **Glue Specified for Jewellery** - Glues like the G-S Hypo Cement and the E6000 are designed particularly for jewelry. The glue sets but remains pliable, so it is less likely to crack and wear off over weeks. The G-S Hypo Cement has a perfect hose, which is perfect for applying a small amount for a smooth finish, alternatively use a cocktail stick to layer the glue.

- **Superglue** - Superglues are extremely rapid glues that can be beneficial, as you do not have to hold up the material until the glue lays. More likely to fire the gel edition, so it is better to be consistent with adding a tiny volume. However, be cautious, as these glues of cyanoacrylate bond skin.

- **Epoxy Resin** - A two-part adhesive very well designed for attaching cords onto metal finds—clean, clean objects with a nail polish remover before adding the glue to avoid greasy fingerprints. A 5-minute epoxy resin reduces the drying period, and as used, one that dries transparent is less likely to become noticeable.

Chapter 2:
Understanding Knots & Mini-Macramé

We will introduce you to some fundamental Macramé knots prior to actually going right into the ventures. It will be the main pillar of Macramé lessons. Furthermore, it will assist you to improve faster through each of the ventures that we will be going through. Generally, there are five specific Macramé knots that you ought to know – both within. You are committed to developing some lovely Macramé items if you focus on making those knots. What you will start finding with these mentioned Macramé knots is that most of the Macramé designs would use one or all of these knots. You will be able to simply get through every Macramé project by trying to learn these simple yet important knots. Furthermore, it will allow you to customize some knots to build your own exclusive Macramé pattern. The five baseline Macramé knots include:

- Lark's Head Knot
- Square Knot
- Berry Knot
- Gathering Knot Double half hitch knot

The above-mentioned knots will be the strings you need to utilize the most often. These are the beginning and finishing ties that you will be incorporating on several of the things you are doing. There are tons of knots you will want to learn, for sure. However, these ties are a decent building block for moving you on the correct track. In case you are not yet acquainted with these five ties, it is suggested that you exercise doing them up several times before you are comfortable with the technique of connecting.

2.1 Different Methods of Tying a Knot

Learn how to tie these basic knots off by core, as they are repeatedly utilized.

 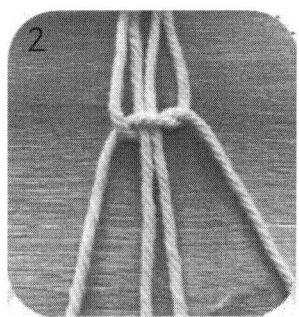

Reef Knot (square)

This is utilized to connect two cord ends of even density and can be loosened by pulling one end back over the knot if needed. It is the foundation in macramé for the square knot.

1. Split cords and lay beside each other so that the two shorter (core) cords are in the center. * carry the right cord underneath the fundamental cords and over the left cord.
2. Take the cord at the leftover of the core cords and transfer it through the loop at the right. Pull the cords to get the knot firm. Repeat from * until the duration needed is in the spiral. To break the loop, adjust the path you tie the knot to.

Square Knot Forms

The square knot is a successful knot used to make macramé bracelets and other paracord items, and the consequent flat knot braid is regarded as Solomon bar. You can deal with new ways to manipulate the simple square knot to produce many appealing variations.

Crossed Cords

To produce a cross-stitch effect, apply a contrast cord color to the base square knot cords, with a flowing stitch design on the reverse side.

1. Begin with an overhand knot and operate one square knot; feed the ends of a variation cord color under the core cords, until you secure the knot.
2. Pass the right-hand comparison chord over the left and lower the key cords to each side of the ears.
3. Perform the first half of the next square knot: left cord underneath the core cords, right cord over the core cords, and bottom through the loop on the left.
4. 4Raise up the cords in comparison over the knots. Perform the second half of the square tie, and then take the correct cord under the contrast cords but over the center cords and the wrong cord. Taking the chord on the left under the contrast cords, through the core cords and Bottom into the loop on the right.
5. Repeat measures 2–4 starting with a cross template. Each time, you can switch the right cord over the left, or alternate for another impact.

Woven Knot Square

Working over the four basic strands, this creates a twisted look Bottom the center of the braid. Ignore the stage directions closely, since each time the cords are not connected like a simple square knot.

1. Knead and rotate a knot overhand. * Bring the left chord above the left core line, behind the right core chord and over the right line. Move the correct cord under both cords as seen, and up through the left cable. Pull ends up the standing firm.
2. Place the right cord under the right core cord, over the left core cord, and below the left cord. Then under all cords, take the left-hand cord and up through the right loop.
3. Continue to repeat from * until braid has the required length. To finish the task, tie a standard knot in the square.

Overhand Knot

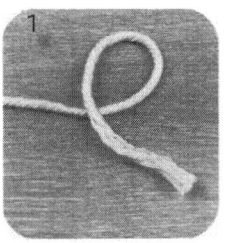 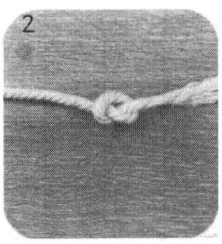 

This basic knot may be attached as a stopper at the end of a rope or as a reminder of the beginning point, or it can be used to detach or connect beads, or simply to create a slipping fastener. Working over the thumb, create a loop in the clockwise direction and, through the loop, pull the working thread up.

Slip Knot

The slipknot is tied to the base of many knotted braids so that the working end is adjustable. Create an anticlockwise loop and keep the string in your left hand at the cross point (below). Place the working cord behind the string, and draw into a U-shaped curve. To change the loop scale, pull the short beginning finish to secure the tie and the working edge.

Lark's Head Knot

This knot is used to tie one cord to another, or to connect a cord to a bar or ring as seen here, and is the most commonly used knot for macramé projects to launch. Split one cord in half, and go around the loop you built from front to back around the pipe. Move the rope around the tails and drawback to close. To create a head knot of a reverse lark, move the rope on the reverse side through the ring and complete the knot again by moving the tails through the circle.

Half-hitch Knot

One of the foundational macramé knots, like shown here, is worked over another cord, or over a ring or bar. It is also used to hold finer cords or threads in pairs. To make a half hitch, take one cord and pass the working end under the other cord and behind the start end. Create a second loop in the same direction around the loop between both the two half hitches to move the job end for extra protection.

Carrick Bend Knot

This knot can be worked on two cords or Utilizing just one thread as explained and it is the basis of many ornamental knots. Start making a loop in one cord in the clockwise direction with the tails on left. Toss the second cord at the bottom right behind the loop, with the starting end. Transfer the working end below the first cord's tails then sew it over and below the cords to come out again at the top of the right loop.

Utilizing Basic Knots

The easiest ties will create the most exquisite jewelry. Overhand knots can be tied to separate or connect beads, and Overhand knots can be connected separately or add beads and reef knots to create a simple and easy bracelet, and there are even other ideas in this segment to bring the best out of common knots.

Overhand Knots

The overhand knot looks awesome wrapped in a rustic leather cord; it can be used for removing beads and adding charms, and for a quick slipping fastening.

1. Use overhand knots to anchor a bead on cord lengths or space beads along leather lengths. Select the cord that correlates to the depth of the bead cavity.

2. One of the strands may be thinner when constructed for two or three cord strands to move through small-hole beads before connecting all the strands together with an overhand knot.

3. Utilize an overhand knot to fasten a charm hop ring or chain around the cord circumference. Bind the knot to the same side of the chain by links to prevent it from twisting.

4. Loop two cord lengths in opposite directions via a washer style bead or button, and then tie each side with an overhand knot to secure it.

5. Make a small beaded tassel by tying a bunch of cords with an overhand knot; add a bead to each strand and tie an overhand knot to secure it above and below the knot.

6. Rest two cords in opposite directions for a sliding fastening and tie an overhand knot over the other cord at each end and firm each. Pull open the tails, and close the main cord.

Reef Knot - Cord too thick for tying intricate knots when working a reef knot can be converted into an easy and efficient design, desirable for making a pretty bracelet.

1. Break two 6 mm chord lengths of 25 cm (10 in), and make a knot of the coral. Change the knot to the same duration on both sides, and softly tug to tighten up.

2. Test the bracelet duration for the fastening, trim the ends of the rope, and fasten all cords to the fastening at either end utilizing solid jewelry glue.

The head-knot of Lark - Sometimes forgotten, this is one of the most popular knots to create jewelry and accessories-the head knots of single or several larks may be used to construct beautiful jewelry designs. In a slide fastening ready to operate a large panel of macramé to create a cuff necklace, the Tie lark's head twists around the loops. Utilizing the head knot of the lark to tie a rope to a sturdy ring to create a pendant, which can be further embellished with bead charms and hop rings. Secure a loop, or another type, with the head knot of a lark on either hand and then secure the ends for a simple bracelet in a fastener.

- **Nesting Lark's head knot** - The head knot of the nesting lark is useful when tangling or working macramé, utilize two cord color schemes. Fasten the head knot of a lark with the first cord (light pink), then lay the second cord (dark pink) laterally under the first knot, take the ends around the back of the base cord and tuck into the created loop.
- **Multiple Lark Head's Knots** - Continue to work the knots one after the other uses a bit distinct methodology, as you will have to stitch one tail across the core cord in order to make the head knot of a lark follow the correct path.

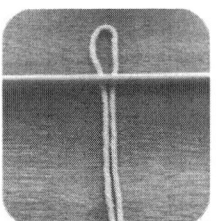  

Single-core technique

1. Use the head knot of a lark to attach a thin cord to one end of a thicker core cord; tie on a second length of thin cord with the head knot of a lark facing in the opposite direction.
2. Work a half hitch over the core cord with the first working-end. Move the job end once more under the core cord and back up through the rope to complete the head knot of a third lark.
3. Start moving from side to side with alternating strings, doing the head knot of one lark at a time. Beads can be inserted Bottom each side of the large loops.

Double Core Technique

1. For the size of a bracelet: tie the head knot of a lark in the center of a thick leather cord that is 40 cm (16 in) wide. Bend this core cord in half, and take over and over the other half of the core cord the top working cord of the lark's head knot.
2. Create a second lark's head knot as Single Core Procedure on the right side of the rope, stage 2, and then diagonally move the right-hand working cord around and over the left-hand heart. Wear the head-knot of a lark. Take the working cord on the left through and over the core cord on the right. Tie the head knot of another larynx.
3. Proceed the crisscross sequence of the head-knots of the lark all the way back Bottom the core cords. The structure of the top loop can be adjusted to fit a button or toggle.

Chinese Knots

Various ethnicities tie knots, but the greatest recognized for their ornamental knots are the Chinese. The connections in this segment are very basic, but others can be combined to construct structures that are more complicated. Sometimes the Chinese ties were connected as symbols of good luck or to protect bad spirits.

Button Knot

Button ties are rather decorative and may be used as an end stopper or as a circular bead instead. Tying with one end of a single cord is seen, so it may also be seen for two cords or a combined chord.

1. Give an anticlockwise loop to the right with the working edge. Create a second anticlockwise loop over the previous, and then keep tightly at the bottom of the chains, at the cross-stage.
2. Weave the job end (right-hand tail) across the two loops from right to left, heading above, below, below, to come out from the other.
3. Carry the working end back around over the beginning edge, move through the circle and through the crossing point, and finish in the center of the knot with the job.
4. Place the bottom loops around your finger, thumb at this stage, and push Bottom the sides to create a ring form or circle around your fingertip. Drag the tails gently to keep them solid.
5. Drag the tails to stretch the tie on the side of the knob before a rope loop emerges. Perform around the knot, pushing Bottom one end of the loop, and pulling through.

6. Continue pressing the knot Bottom immediately, continuing to work in the same direction across the button knot until one end reaches it. Take out your finger and continue the procedure of removing the rope until the knot is secure.

Moving a button knot

It could be challenging to place them precisely when required to work button knots beside each other or next to a bead, so this technique allows you to move one knot to another.

1. Attach the first button knot to the right position, then plug a second button knot to end up close to the first but do not pull it too tightly.
2. Switch the knot around until you reach the loop on the left-hand side that appears as the main rope, and pull the loop around until the second button knot is pushed over to butt up to the first.
3. Function through the knot dragging parallel loops through until you meet the working rope at the other end, repeated the knot to make it the same size as the first knot, if possible. Attach further knots of the ring, and then push them along the string.

Sliding Button Knot Fastening

Utilizing button ties to fasten a necklace or bracelet with a stylish slipping release. Different string colors are highlighted for clearness, but the cords should be the same color for a necklace or bracelet.

1. Fasten a button knot to the toggle stage at the end of the chord (see Knot switch, step 4). Pass the other end of the cord (shown here in contrast color) through the center of the toggle in the opposite direction to the short tail, then pull loops through the button knot (see button knot, steps 5 and 6) to make a small firm knot.

2. Arrange on the left side the first button knot with a long end of the other cord out to the right. Start by wrapping the first two loops around the other chord in the anticlockwise direction (shown here in contrast color).

3. Continue to finish the knot on the button and then work through the loops to firm the second knot around the other cord. Pull the knots to close the attachment, and open the main cords.

4. Inside the second button knot, apply a little glue where the tail arises and trim when dry, then secure the first knot in the same manner. Make sure the ties on the click are slipping while the glue dries.

Knot on the double coin

The double coin knot is a variant of the Carrick turn, and its form imitates a traditional Chinese style pattern with two ancient coins that converge.

1. Make a loop in a clockwise direction at least 20 cm (8 in) from the cord's starting end, so the cross point is on the left.

2. Holding the cross point in your left hand will bring the end of the workaround so that it will form a U-shaped bend to finish running Bottom the loop.

3. Change to retain the loops in your right hand and work end cord. Pass the work-end as shown under the start-end.

4. Weave the tail of the job stopping above, below, over and under the cords to emerge from the correct coil.

5. Pull the job end through so all three loops are of the same thickness until you start forming the knot. If a soft cord or a somewhat frayed end is used, build a U-shaped bend with the functioning end before winding it through the loops in phase 4.

6. Change to build a relatively loose knot, which is tight enough to remain secure by removing the ends and working the cord through.

Carrick bends double coin knot

Start with a double coin knot and then work a series of Carrick bends to develop a wide knotted band, modifying the spacing between them as you wish.

1. Start with a long cord in the center and tie a double coin knot (see Double Coin Knot). Make the right cord an anticlockwise loop, place the left cord Bottom across the loop and hold where the cords cross.

2. Put the left cord under the right cord to complete the first Carrick bent and then Bottom the gap under the double coin knot. Weave through the chains below, over and beneath.

3. Firm up, adjusting the length between the knots of the 'legs' Start tie the next Carrick bend on the left cord with a clockwise loop and lay the right cord over the top. Change the starting direction of each knot until the required length is reached.

Toggle

The toggle is a variant of the head knot of a Turk operating from the base of a double coin knot, and its size may differ based on the length of the cord and the amount of times the cord is threaded through.

1. Tie a knot of the double coin (see Double Coin Knot) such that the beginning end of the left hand is low, and the working end of the right hand is wider. Bring the end of the workaround and return it back through the first loop where the end of the start arises.
2. Taking the same direction as the beginning point, thread the working point below, repeatedly, to arise from the other side of the loops and drag it over the right-hand loop bottom.
3. Take the functioning cord around and begin to take the beginning end direction like in stage 2, holding the cord inwards when you move along. Proceed until all the cords have doubled up.
4. Place your finger in the center of the knot at this stage and keep between your finger and thumb, so that it creates a loop rather than a flat knot. Drag the thread between the two ends to have the toggle closed.

The Prosperity Knot

Because this knot represents many double coin knots that have been operating together, it is said to carry riches and fortune to everyone who binds or combines it into their garments.

1. Start by binding a double coin knot in the middle of a cord length (see Double Coin Knot). Pull the side loops out from each side one at a time to about 3 cm (1 1/4 in) (this will differ depending on the density of your cord).

2. Bring the loops Bottom on either side underneath the working ends, and modify the twirling at the highest point of the knot to be firm.

3. Carrying the operating ends out of the way where the left hand on each of the long loops bends into the center.

4. Tuck the loop on the left, right up through the back of the loop. Bring the right end of the work Bottom and under the top loop, so it lies between the two twisted loops.

5. Wrap the twisted top loop Bottomward into the twisted loop below to catch the end of the job. The knot cords are re-adjusted to make the knot much more so.

6. Carry the left working end Bottom and up in the middle of the left side, through the remaining loop. Weave over, under, over, and under to get out to the right. Set the knot until the firm.

Macramé Multi-strand

For multiple cords other than the simple four, you can operate macramé to build broader fringing loops, a belt, or a cuff bracelet. Multistrand macramé could even be used in the round to produce items like bags or crop holders. However, you have to prepare ahead of more than four cords, figure out the layout, the number of cords needed, and how to protect them from getting going.

Switching square ties

While you may operate a square knot over a single cord (totally three cords), it is easier to work with fractions of four base cords for alternating square knots.

1. Set the macramé cords-the the doubled-over cords were attached to board here. Attach a second cord to each pair of cords utilize an overhand knot, and rotate for a tidier finish.
2. Connect the first four cords then create a square knot for the next four cords. Work through the cords attaching one square knot on each four-cord party before you meet the end of the string. Push the taut ties, so they do not get free.
3. The operating cords from the previous row would become the core cords on the next row and vice versa. Split the first two cables, and then attach them to the side. Differentiate the next four cords and set a square knot to work.
4. Run through the cords forming a square knot on every four-cord party before you meet the last two cords on the left side.
5. We take the two spare cords Bottom to the next side. Perform the next row as the first row from right to left, putting a square knot on the first four cords, and on every four cords around the row.
6. To design the macramé panel, continue to repeat the tying pattern in two-rows. Try to tie knots each time for one even panel to the same spacing, Utilizing pins to maintain the panel as you move Bottom.

Straight half-hitch rib

Typically used as a double half hitch in pairs, the half hitches are generally employed along one of the side cords to create a dense horizontal rib as seen. \

1. Arrange one of the outer strings horizontally over the other cables. Take the existing vertical outer cord to the right above the horizontal cord and then below it again.
2. Use the same chord over the horizontal chord, and this time bring it across the circle on the right leg. Replicate the two ties in conjunction for each of the vertical cords to build a dense rope. Bring the inner cord back over the vertical cables, and reverse the cycle in the opposite direction until you meet the top.

Half-hitch rib with Angled-edge

Half hitches are also used to render form sided tables. Each hand cord is taken back and forth to operate straight half hitch, so if you use consecutive cords on a specified leg, the tip is bent instead.

1. Hook right cable over other vertical cords—function along this central cord a row of half-hitch rope, joining double half hitches with each vertical cable. Click the next chord at just below the arm. Function a half-hitch rib line over the current core cord ending with a double half hitch on the left-hand side over the old core chord.
2. In the next right-hand cord under the rib and function another half-hitch path-the the panel has already begun to form

diagonally. Think of functioning half hitches at the end of each row over the previous core thread.

3. To adjust the course by making apiece by macramé that zigzags, take the new central cord and push it back over the vertical cords to the right. Repeat steps 1 and 2, except now take the next cord to the left to operate each chain.

Half-hitch ribs for the diagonal pattern can be worked at an angle, and they can even be used to create shapes such as leaves and petals. Although most macramé techniques use the double half hitch, knotted designs can be produced Utilizing single half hitches too.

Diagonal Half hitch

The core cord is pinned straight across by creating a horizontal rib, so if the core cord is pinned at an angle, a diagonal rib across, however, if the core cord is pinned at an angle, a diagonal rib is made.

1. Practice One half-hitch rib row around the cords. Attach a button to the rib edge. Wrap the side (core) cord around the pin at the angle you want to make, then over the vertical cord. Insert a pin to protect the string at its root.
2. In addition, add two half hitches with each vertical cord to make sure that you hold the rib diagonal while you tighten up the ties. Ensure that the longitudinal cords above the diagonal rib are not too loose or close and that they lay flat.
3. Simply pin the core cord diagonally in the opposite direction to create a zigzag, and work half hitches again with all vertical

cords. Use the same core cord at the end of the row to go back in the opposite direction once more.

Petal Shapes

With a little forward thought, basic forms of half-hitch ribs can be built in all kinds. Here the rib angle and the spacing have created a petal shape – use the method to try out other patterns.

1. Pull the right-hand core cord, and then push it over the vertical cords and snap, so that the core cord has a gentle upward curve. Task half hitches around the cord, changing each knot to hold the curve running.

2. Bend the central cord around a pin on the left, then in a Bottomward curve around the vertical cords to create the petal form. Hook half hitches over the middle cord to complete the form of the petal.

Endless fall

Because it has the appearance of a waterfall, the first of the single half-hitch variations is so named, and the vertical cords seem to flow over and fall behind horizontal crossed cords.

1. Fold around a pin with one cord in half, with the U-shaped bend at the tip. Place the second cord behind you, then function from its midpoint, pass over the ends, first left, then right, until they overlap.

2. Bring the vertical (blue) cords up one at a time and form a half-hitch knot behind the crossed-over (beige) cords in such a manner that the tails end up face Bottom in between.

3. Repeat cord crossing and joining of half hitches until the braid has the appropriate length. Gently draw the cords crossed so that the half hitches are secure. Change the loop at the top of the macramé to create a simple and easy cuff, so that it is the perfect size for a toggle or button fastening string.

Endless Side-By-Side Falls

The two rope shades are bound together in a subtly different manner to create a bright line around the duration with this type of infinite drop.

1. Create a circle in the center of one (blue) string such that the left end is finished. Place the second (beige) cord above the cross-stage, around the circle.

2. Place the right end of the loop (blue) cord around the ring, and then lock the second (beige) cord into the newly created ring to the right. To tie up the slipknot, take the first (blue) chord and alternately organize the chord colors.

3. Conduct as with Endless Falls, such as the vertical colors on each side of the braid, is distinct. The cables at the intersection will move from hand to hand.

Chain-link Endless falls

By Utilizing the endless fall method, a particular design and pattern may be produced by utilizing four or more vertical cords-only operate for an even amount of cords.

1. Start with Endless Falls Working Stages 1 and 2. Feed a third (brown) cord over the two half-hitches and over horizontal (beige) cords Bottom through each side of the crossed. Push the cords crossed to keep the knot tight.
2. Turn over the horizontal (beige) cords, right over left again. Work half hitches with all four vertical cords, taking each cord Bottom on the half-hitch right-hand side. Pull the side cords horizontally to make the knot firm.
3. Repeat step 2, but this time take each half hitch with the vertical cords Bottom on the left side. Continue to repeat these two rows until the braid is the required length, lowering back to two half hitches at the end.

Attach Beads to Macramé

Although macramé is an unadorned and elegant knotting tool, it can be quickly embellished with beads and jewels to produce different types. Some of the most common techniques for embellished macramé is the Shamballa-style bracelets with sparkly beads inserted into a single row of square knots.

Apply Beads to Cords

1. Stringing all the beads onto the core cords at once is simpler than inserting the beads one at a time as desired.

2. Function first segment of macramé over single or double core strings, depending on the depth of the bead opening. Attach the pin, and then fasten the string with a spring clip at the bottom of the plate.

3. Move the first bead to the end knot. Carry both sides of the bead Bottom the working cords and create a square knot underneath. You may operate one or two ties in the square between the beads.

4. Begin to operate the ties before the macramé bends to carry the functioning cords back to the sides before inserting a bead.

5. Apply beads to the operating cords. The beads should be smaller by attaching beads to the functioning strings, as there is just one continuous string of rope to travel between them.

6. Beads are attached while you operate, so move them up to the previous knot by applying just the beads you need to each working rope.

7. Workaround the core cords like before with the next macramé knot. After each knot continues to add beads to the outer working cords.

The outer working cords are transferred directly on a larger mass of macramé to the next row of knots. You should attach a bead to the next row of ties on each of those cords. To make an appealing edging, you should put a bead on each of those strings.

Finishing Techniques

Knotting methods often have at minimum one raw end to render a piece of clothing, necklace, or other objects that needs to be softened or protected in any way. Common methods such as whipping or button knots utilize the knotting rope itself to cover the raw ends, or you may use a large range of specifically made tools and fastenings for this function.

Nipping the Bad Ends

Cords and braids appear to splay out at the top, so it is important that the top is neatened to a degree so that you can make it into a find. There are different techniques that you may use to loosen raw ends, but which one you select depends on the number of strands and the form of product used.

The Combination

In Utilizing nylon knotting rope or paracord, first neaten the end by keeping it in a flame for a second or two-a kitchen gas lighter is enough-to heat the end and connect the raw ends. Please take note not to flame your fingertips while burning the ends of the string with a gaslighter.

Wrap Up

Utilizing solid beading or sewing thread, or fine wire, when adding a finding to finish braids or rope ends. This method gives no added thickness to the thread.

1. Function next to the end of the rope, carefully tie the string or wire around to the end of the rope such that the covering is even, and the beginning point is stuck below. Do not overwrap because that is going to be too thick.

2. Stitch the tail under the twisted fibers utilizing a sewing needle. Trim the neck, and often over the top of the cord where appropriate.

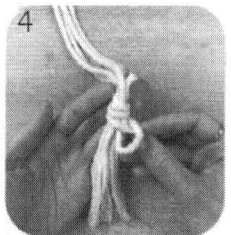 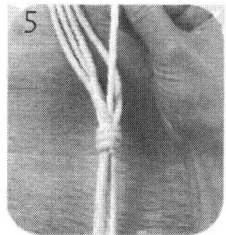 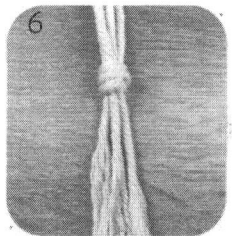

Whip-off

A stronger rope should be used with a glamorous whipped finish. This method may also be used for making a loop on a single end or around a double cord, as seen here.

1. Develop a thin cord loop at the end of the braid or looped braid and place it on top edge. From the bottom coil, the working end through the braid, then many times around all loop cords.

2. Continue wrapping the fine cord to shape a single wrapping width. Holding the cords clean and tidy when binding, but the end of the job into the circle.

3. Drag the thin cord loop tail softly, and then pull to cover the rope under the whipping. Trim all sleeveless tops.

Finishing With Ends of the Cord, End Caps and Cones

There are lots of various string end, end cap or cone types, and designs appropriate for finishing raw ends, and some of the large variety is discussed in String ends and end caps. Cord ends are tiny metal finds crafted to cover one or more raw edges. End caps that may be a rectangle, rectangular or circular, are wider than the ends of the cord and ideal for a thick rope or braid. Both sides have either a solid ring or hole for attachment of a fastening. The internal distance or length of the sample must be compared to the thickness or duration of the string or braid and end cone or cap connected.

1. Cover the end of the braid (or string bundle) with a fine stitching or beading thread (see Wrap Up), make sure that the Wrapping is not too thick to conceal within the end cap; cut easily.

2. Smear a thin adhesive (E6000 or G-S Hypo Cement) across the inner rim of the end cap Utilizing a cocktail stick, even placing a drop or two inside at the edge. Stop putting a strain on the finding outside.

3. Press the braid (or cords) into the end cap to ensure sure it is straight, so no raw ends are protruding; you may use a pin from a dressmaker to tuck some leftover fibers away. Repeat at the other end and leave for 24 hours to recover.

Attach a Ring to a Tail Cone or Cap

Many end cone or cap types have a hole at the top, instead of a rim. You may connect a strip of wire or a headpin to the braid and then create a twisted or simple cord. Use the design to match the process, so that the raw ends are hidden, and the end cap or cone edge snugly wraps through the braid or cords.

1. Cover or whip the end of the braid or set of threaded or delicate wire strings to ensure sure the end cap always stays on. Bend the headpin from the end over around 6 mm (⁄ in) and push under the cover.
2. Pull the headpin end out into the braid end center. Use snipe-nose pliers to bend the headpin end back over the Wrapping towards the end of the braid.
3. Add glue or cone inside the end cap and insert the braid through the hole feeding the headpin.
4. Work a straight loop at headpin end. If the hole is wide, you should apply a tiny bead before creating the circle, to plug the void.

The Final Touches

Starting macramé and other methods of knotting is always tied with a rope or into a fastening, so there are no raw ends. Yet the result of the job still has beginnings to complete. If the architecture allows, you can simply leave a fringe, or use one of many finishing techniques. Some glues dry out and become fragile, but jewelry glue like E6000 or G-S Hypo Cement should remain pliable until dry for a more stable and sturdy attach.

1. Utilizing a cocktail stick or a small nozzle adhesive tube to add a little adhesive under the end cords as it exits from the final knot. Leave on to dry for 24 hours.

2. Verify the ends of the cord are secure. For cotton wax ties, cut around the knot.

3. When you use a nylon string, such as the Chinese knotting rope, cut a little farther away and then melt the end cautiously with a tiny flame.

2.2 Tips and Techniques for Better Knotting

If you are a novice, then review a few attributes you should remember while selecting your macramé string.

Composition

The product from which the macramé cord was created is very essential. Fibers like hemp and jute used to be highly popular among macramé makers. However, their consumer presence motivated the increase in popularity of nylon, and satin ray produced macramé strings, which are man-crafted fibers. It is recommended that you use nylon as a novice since it is simple to undo in case you create a knotting failure.

Strength

A macramé cord's strength primarily depends on how it was formed. A cord made of jute, leather, ribbon, and nylon is sturdy enough.

Twist

The strength of the rope is calculated by the twisting or braiding of the different strands of the thread during the production phase. A woven macramé rope is less likely to undo than a twisted string. Always regard the edges of a cord before actually starting a macramé project so you can avoid the stands from segregating. The strands can be dipped in clear liquefied wax. If you wish to build a fringe, guarantee that the threads do not break past the duration of the fringe by fastening the tip of the fringe.

Stiffness

A cord must be versatile enough to curl and stretch as per the specifications of the design. If you are attempting to create a necklace or bracelet, it is suggested to use a slimmer macramé chain. An embroidery cord crafted from cotton, for instance, is smooth and very durable. You may also use leather just to ensure that the width is less than 2 mm.

Finish or Surface

There are macramé strings that render the skin sound rough and can be uncomfortable. Necklaces and bracelets like that are not approved for producing hemp and metallic strings. The products recommended for use are mostly silk, nylon, satin rayon, and cotton. You may also use leather, but after a time of usage, it loosens.

Diameter or distance

Typically specifies the length of the macramé cord in millimeters (mm). While buying a cord, please remember that they may be incorporated into buttons, pins, or other accessories. Cords with diameters greater than 4.0 mm can need greater decorations. An excellent-size cord will have a diameter of less than 2.0 mm for producing micro-macramé items, such as necklaces or bracelets.

Sum or quantity

The quantity of cord corresponds to the extending capability of the cord required for the whole task. Many cords come in wide rolls, whereas others arrive in shorter pieces.

Most customers use cords of nylon and cloth since they are searching for one of the highest performing macramé creators. In addition, because these particular cords are better and easily available in the market.

Measurement Required For Project Completion

It would require some forethought to finish your Macramé project because you cannot just terminate the project and leave it crumbling. When you learn how long the ends are meant to last, you should cut them off. There are various methods to finish the cording, and each Macramé design should have its own directions. "Wrapping" is one method where you will finish a set of loose strings. Wrapping is achieved by taking one of the current strings and wrapping around the other. Many cord-cutting methods include:

- Utilizing the Overhand Knots set, with one knot at the center.
- A line of beads keeping an Overhand Knot in place.
- An alternate Half Hitch knot is included.
- Unraveling the end strings and sagging them by untangling their folds.

Another method for completing the job is to braid three or four cords and then keep them with an Overhand Knot in place. Twist two or more chord sets in a clockwise direction, and then twist the groups in a counterclockwise direction. Hook an Overhand Tie together to secure the twists. You should twist the cording in the same direction as the initial twist to get a more gnarled look before it twists in irregular shapes. You may also use Monkey's Fist Knots sequence. You should use a Clove Hitch over a horizontal bar for a stable end without any hanging strings, then put the ends up to the back of the job and tie them in the knots. Then you should tie or bind the ends, so they fit securely. In certain instances, each Macramé project should contain guidance about how to bind and end the job.

Anchoring the Idea As You Are Working

It is crucial that when you are working, you hold your Macramé project securely rooted in place. You will want to tie the ends of the cord utilizing some form of an anchor. The advantages of keeping career anchored include:

- You can keep the cords close and stable. This contributes to consistent and accurate Macramé functions in both tightness and thickness.
- Cables remain untangled and are simple to use.
- You should retain stress even through the whole job.
- You are supposed to keep track of what step you are going to take next.

One way to keep the work stabilized is by utilizing a Macramé frame. Utilize pins to connect cording ends to the wall. Be sure the ends of the cording are positioned in such a way that the job is as clean and standard as the end of the project launch.

Another way to secure the cording is with a quick clipboard. A clipboard will encourage you to go along your project steps as well as store the unfinished piece if you do not operate on it. The cording remains clean and tidy until you can resume work. It is quick to use a clipboard: lock the cord under the frame, enabling the cords to hang free. You should attach them to the clipboard Utilizing tape if you are dealing with center cords. A split ring is yet another way to stabilize and hold your work safe. Drop the knot into the split ring slot after you have formed your starting knot. Then loop the ring onto a secure item, like a doorknob or a chain for garments. You will be forced to split some strands twice as long as others do for certain designs. Everything you need to do in this situation is a loop cord fold over the top of the band. Everything you need to do when you are about to fix the ties is separate the whole project from the loop.

Leveling Up Your Work

The start and the end ties of your design may need to be twisted such that the ends are tightly fixed. A convenient way to achieve this is to use pliers. Keep growing cording string, with the point of the pliers, a few now. Stiffen the threads tightly by pushing the pliers out from the cording. This should make your Macramé project better, and it stays healthy and stable.

Holding your work stable and balances

You will want to concentrate ever more on making your job smooth and consistent as you get more advanced in Macramé painting. You will also want friction to be reasonable and the knots line to be horizontally, vertically, and diagonally clear. You will be aiming for solid points, and sometimes chains. Through Utilizing the Macramé frame, or other anchoring techniques, the simplest and most effective way to accomplish this excellence is to protect your job whilst you are functioning. The Macramé board should help keep your ties uniformly spaced and your project template uniform. Before you tie the first knot, get into the habit of protecting your job. You will soon notice that even with ties that match and are the same size, the Macramé creations feel.

2.3 Creating Ornaments and Accessories with Macramé

Macramé has been there for centuries as a conventional profession but this knotting practice has taken the headlines in recent times. Used to build elegant wall hangings that will spruce up in every house, did you know you could produce cute mini macramé for jewelry with the correct equipment? Better part? To achieve the classic macramé feel, you do not even have to use complicated knots. Here is how to go about it.

Butterfly Pin Utilizing Macramé

This butterfly pin is simple and simple to create and is a perfect option for beginners. It is so simple that you could make more than one, and even parcel it over to your friends and relatives.

<u>Supplies</u>

- Adhesive/Glue
- Feet 1 mm Hemp
- Wooden beads, with an inch size of 1/4
- Masking tape
- Craft pin for jewelry

<u>Guidelines for creating</u>

1. Break the hemp rope into three 12-inch sections each.
2. Split in half on the cords and add the folded end to the surface, or attach to the Macramé plate.
3. Slip a bead onto the string, pulling it out from the fold to about 2

4. Position the other two cord strands to close, and then slip under the folded strands below the bead.

5. Get a Square Knot tight up to the bead utilizing the double cording string?

6. Create another Square Knot from the first knot, around 1⁄2 inch. Push up the knot to meet the first knot. That will shape the butterfly's top wings.

7. Slide the other two beads through the cording.

8. Create a final Square Knot from the last bead about 1⁄2 inch apart. Move the knot up to the final bead to shape the butterfly's bottom wings.

9. Position the Last Square Knot with a little dollop of glue on. Let this dry up entirely.

10. Split twin threads next to the last knot.

11. Cut the anchoring rope from the last tie, around 3/8 of an inch.

12. Rip the tapes off.

13. At the fold, the folding cords break.

14. Knead a knot in each cord to create the butterfly antenna.

15. Cut close to knots.

16. Glue the assembled butterfly onto the pin.

Stone armbands Utilizing Macramé

Micro macramé made with a fine knotting cord makes delicate jewelry is which is phenomenal.   To make a plain beaded bracelet, beads can be adorned to the outer part of the cords, or add a little piece of jewelry by tangling the cords around the rhinestone cup chain.

<u>Supplies:</u>

- Glue (Particularly E6000 used for Jewelry)
- Rhinestone (or any other stone) cup chain 11 cm (4 / in) of 4 mm (stretched out)
- 2.5 m (2 / yd.) 1 mm nylon knotting string
- Board and pins (optional)

How to Create

1. Split the knotting cord to a length of 50 cm (20 in), then divide all parts in half. Pin or tie the limited duration of the string overhead to the work board. Attach the longer article of cord to an overhand knot across the small side.

2. Deal with 3 cm (one / in) of square knots for a 17.5 cm (7 in) long bracelet to retain the knots in position at the bottom.

3. Place the weight of the cup chain over the fibers of the two strings. Perform a square knot on the cup chain after each rhinestone. Look at the top of the original square knot to check where the bar is: if it is on the right, then continue the next square knot with the correct rope; if it is on the bottom, continue with the bottom string. Continue to work a square knot for each rhinestone, rotating the side you start the knot to hold the knots in place.

4. Complete the macramé with a segment of square knots 3 cm (1/ in) or function the duration to suit the other end. Test the bracelet size, and change if appropriate. Act over two cords with a two-strand button tie, winding the cords in pairs. Gradually strengthen the button knot, pushing the cords in, so that it lies from the square knots around 3–5 mm (u –/ in).

5. Apply a small adhesive within the knot of the button where the cords appear at the core and prune the cords once the adhesive has hardened. Test that the loop at the opposite end of the cuff fits nicely over the knot ring. You can alter a little by dragging Bottom or up the center core cords of the macramé knots. To

hold the loop to the appropriate dimension, add a little adhesive on the opposite side.

Brooch Utilizing Macramé

Macramé is sometimes thought of as a very simple wrinkly knotting tool, but it turns into a rather sophisticated micro macramé when used in delicate cords. To build a mosaic effect through this gorgeous brooch, use matching colors.

<u>Supplies</u>

- Core Foam surface
- 20 cm (8 in) of 1 mm (19swg) of half a hard silver sterling wire

- Seed beads: size six (3.5 mm) of matt silver, size 10 (2 mm) of polished peach, size 11 (2.2 mm) of silver crystal, and gold luster of smart raspberry.
- Map pins
- Ultrasuede10 cm (4 in) sq.
- Sticky tape
- Each SuperlonTM cord is 1.5 m (1/2 yd.) in teal, royal blue, turquoise, white and scarlet pink
- The Tools of Jewelry Brooch Back
- Hose and thread

How to Create

1. Buckle the silver wire in the quarter to create a 'V' form that ended slightly oval. Get the SuperlonTM cables ready for use: red, lilac, blue, light gray, and dusky black.
2. Carry on the teal cord, a silver-lined crystal seed bead, and slide Bottom to the middle. Fold the cord in half, and then position it on one side of the 'V' over the cable. Taking the tails over the wire and through the loop back to create the head knot of a reverse lark
3. Work on both sides of a half hitch. To the other colored cords, replicate measures 2 and 3, inserting a bead each cycle.
4. Place the outline of the wire on the center of the foam board and bring the tape into place. * Bring the lilac end chord in parallel to the thread. Act with each cord in effect a double half hitch (see Multistrand Macramé: straight half-hitch Rib).

5. Place a map pin at the edge of the rib, and push the purple cord back at a small angle via the vertical cords. Safe with tape or snap on a leaf. Act for the dusky pink cords and the first black cable in double half hitches. On the next grey thread, pick up a color-lined peach seed bead and again operate double half hitches.

6. Perform the first coral cord with double half-hitches, then pick up two silver-lined crystal seed beads on the next coral string; lock with double half-hitches; For the first lilac thread, add three emerald raspberry gold lustre seed beads, locking again with double half-hitches.

7. Finally ending with a silver-lined crystal, a size six matte silver and a silver-lined crystal on the remaining purple thread, perform double half hitches on the next lilac thread. Run the remaining half hitch of the pair.

8. Repeat six to seven times from *, depending on the strain, before the macramé coils across the semicircle to touch the wire again. Yet again bringing the purple cord back to the outside side, operating straight half-hitch arm. Function double half hitches over the wire for any chord in place.

9. Wrap all the tails in the rope under the silver cable. Pick up two silver-lined crystals on the first dusky pink chain, one size six matte silver seed bead, and two silver-lined crystals. Work on the other side of the wire 'V' shape a double half hitch. Fasten the next light dusky string without beads. Repeat on the two grey cords and then work the wire Bottom, adding ornaments

with the first of each hue, decreasing the number of silver-lined beads as the gap between the wires narrows.

10. Function a macramé semicircle to suit the first leg, and finish with a simple half-hitch arm. Start on the first cord a double half-hitch, then attach a silver-lined stone. To hold the beadwork, another double half-hitch with the same thread. Sync with each chord in second.

11. Cover the rope ends with small stitching around the back of the macramé and thread it invisibly. Trim sparingly. Cut UltrasuedeTM into position invisibly along the edge to match any semicircle and thread.

12. Stitch a brooch over on the one hand on the back of the brooch, sewing straight through on the other hand, and going around to the back so that the small thread between the macramé knots is concealed inside. Sew the ends tightly onto.

Tassel Macramé Earring

Now we are approaching one of your favorite macramé designs-earrings. Most precisely, earrings with tassels. If you are searching for motivation and designs for your next macramé design, don't look any further as the macramé earrings are a perfect beginner-friendly endeavor for which you can get started quickly.

Macramé earrings are quick to create and ideal for any occasion. You should wear them as a sign of design, combining them and adding them to specific accessories. It is a perfect place to show off your own particular personality and artistry. You should spend around 45 min-1 hour, producing them for this macramé project. In this job, you can need just two knots-a double half-hitch knot and an over-hand knot. For this project, you would most definitely need to get some macramé string and a pair of hoop earrings. If earrings fascinate you, make sure to send this DIY macramé hack a try.

Macramé Supply Requirements:

- 1 mm String Cotton
- Embroidery String
- Earrings

Cotton Cord Length:

- Cords 6 x (3″-5″) (for one earring)
- Embroidery Line longitude:
- 1 x 22″ (for an ornament only)

2.4 Frequently Asked Questions about macramé

Now that you have understood the basics of Macramé and how it works, here is a small section that will cover the Frequently Asked Questions to resolve any query you have.

What is the ideal cord for macramé?

It hinges on your idea. The 5 mm 3 plies twisted cotton cord is usually a best-seller. Working with it is simple; it is incredibly durable and sturdy and unravels to create a very lovely fringe at the ends.

The string is another powerful element. It is a little less strong than the chain, and you may not want to create furniture from it, but on the paws, this fiber is much smoother. Even our string is perfect for other crafts such as sewing, spinning, creating jewelry, and more.

Are rope and cords different

Certainly, the words are always interchanged, so there is no major distinction. The cord is a more general word that can be extended to a number of long-stranded materials. They can be bent, braided, or spun, or not. The rope comes under the rope umbrella, which requires winding, braiding, or stitching several fibers together to create a workable rope.

How much rope to my venture do I need?

It depends upon how thick the knotting is going to be. When you are creating a looser board, it is recommended you want 4x the piece's finished weight. And if you want your hanging wall to be 3 feet tall, then subtract it by 4. You're going to want to split rope by 12 centimeters. When you are creating something more complex, closely knotted, or with little negative room, reducing the length of your ideal finished piece by 6x is advised.

Chapter 3:
Macramé Projects for Indoors

The perfect way to give the Boho touch to your space is by Macramé DIY Projects. It often helps you pay less and the greatest thing of that is they will be perfect presents for those you love. Does not matter what you are searching for, whether it is your own personalized Gift idea for your mom on mother's day, or your spouse on Valentine's Day or anniversary, these Macramé projects are always exceptional for your indoors.

3.1 Macramé Wall & Door Hangings

A hung macramé wall is a simple DIY project that will bring a personalized touch to every space within your house. This free tutorial can allow you to build a wall hanging with several fun designs, including spirals and triangles. Do not worry about changing it up to make it your own.

Notwithstanding how it sounds, this straightforward project only requires one or two hours to finish. It always comes together easily, and you will notice many ways to introduce your own theme. The knots that you are going to use for hanging this macramé wall contain Lark's Head Knot, Spiral Knot, and Square Knot. By reading the instructions mentioned here on how to macramé, you can learn how to tie all those knots.

Requirements

- Cotton Macramé Cord (61 m or 200 feet)
- Wood Dowel (3/4 "diameter, 24" long)
- Scissors

How to Create

1. The wooden dowel should not be such exact proportions, so choose any scale you want in place of the wooden dowel as long as you can accommodate all the ropes over it. If you choose to give it a more natural look, a tree branch around the same size may be used.
2. Make your wooden dowel a hanger.
3. A macramé string attached to a wooden dowel with scissors next to it.
4. Cut a three-foot (one meter) length of macramé thread. Add each end of the cord to the wooden dowel on both sides.

5. Macramé thread sliced into pieces utilizing a pair of scissors.

6. Split the macramé string into 12 rope pieces, which are 15 foot wide (4.5 meters).

7. It may seem like a ton of rope, but knots take up more string than you thought. There is no way to make the rope thicker if you need to, but taking further is easier than Utilizing.

8. Fold one of the macramé cords in two, and then tie it to the wooden dowel utilizing the head knot of a lark. Likewise, add such strings.

9. Take the first four cords and create a spiral stitch to the left (also called a half-knot Sinnet) by making 13 half knots.

10. Utilizing the next package of four ropes to perform another 13, half knots spiral stitch. Keep operating in 4-cord parties. You should have six spiral-stitches when you finish.

11. Measure about two inches Bottom in spiral stitch from the last knot. It is where the next knot, the square knot, would be placed.

12. Create a right-facing square tie, utilizing the first four strings. Go across this row, rendering the correct square knots faced. Do the utmost to bring both of them placed horizontally linked. You are going to wind up with six square knots in the band.

13. Then it is time to start decreasing the square knots, and we can get a "V" knots form.

14. Leave the two cords first, and the two cords last secure. Create square ties facing each set of four to the right. You will also have a second row of unknotted two first and two last strings, and five square knots.

15. It does not matter if you spread these out; just hold them for each row and for each other.

16. You must cut out the first four cords for the third section, and the remaining four cords. You are going to have four knots in the square.

17. Take out six cords at the start for the fourth section, and six cords at the top. You are going to get three knots in the line.

18. In the fifth section, at the top, you can cut out eight cords and, in the end, eight cords more. Now you should have two knots in the line.

19. You will cut out ten cords at the start for the sixth and final section, and ten cords at the top. This will leave you with four cords to make a final knot in the square.

20. Time to bring on some square ties. We will be growing them this time to shape a triangle, like an upside-Bottom "V."

21. Take out the first eight and last eight cords to the first row of this segment. You are going to create two knots in the line.

22. Leave out six cords at the beginning and end in the third section. Within this row, you should have three knots within the line.

23. Take out four cords at the beginning of the fourth section, and four at the top. You are going to have four knots in the square.

24. Take out at the start two cords in the fifth section, and the last two cords. Now in this row, you should have five knots in the line.

25. Use all the cords to make knots to the last row. With this row, you should have six knots in the line.

26. Time to put a good trim on your macramé board. Leave some room beneath the final row (six to eight inches or so). Utilizing the scissors to the right through the strings.

27. You may keep it as if it is, connect any pins, fray the ends, or make basic knots overhand as above.

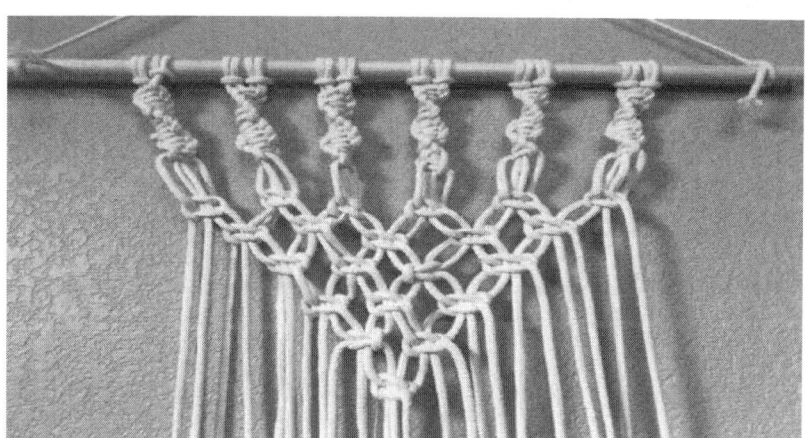

Dream Catcher

This surrealistic Macramé creation is perfect to create as a treat for somebody dear to you.

<u>Requirements</u>

- Feathers
- A 4 "brass ring
- 6 yards of any specific cording kind, 2 mm in size
- 15 Pony beads

<u>How to Create</u>

1. Attach the brass ring to one edge of the cording.
2. Loop the cording around the chain, ensuring sure to pull firmly after each loop. To begin the next web row, simply loop the cord around the first cord and drop. Start looping until the target size is the gap in the middle.

3. You can attach the beads anywhere in the pattern when creating the dream catcher. Loop the cord just before inserting the bead, and then move the cord into the bead. The bead is then placed within the design's site.

4. When the site design is growing, you are able to use the cording to cover the frame—utilizing a Double Knot to lock one end of the chain. Cover the ring length with the cording, and then connect the ends to be stable.

5. Split a 6-8 inch long piece of cording. Attach the beads anywhere you want and make sure you attach a Double Knot after the last bead. Move a feather via the beads before snugly placed. Utilizing a Double Knot to tie the rope to the loop.

6. Utilize an outer sheath of 6-inch cording, attached to the base of the dream catcher, to mount the finished product.

Macramé feathers

If you are trying to bring more depth and shading to your macramé designs, there is no better way than by incorporating feathers. The feathers may also be made into basic key chains, earrings, charms, or other jewelry.

Three different macramé feather designs are exchanged with this novice DIY macramé project, and you can use them to integrate into your bigger macramé creations or to use them as a feather charm. Owing to the soft fringe and shine, Macramé feathers look distinctive. When you see a macramé project adorned with feathers and leaves, it is hard not to pause and take a second glance. Many love a piece of feathers, leaves, and are fascinated to know how to incorporate them in their macramé journey at some stage.

When you are going to use the macramé creations and ventures to create a point, there is no easier way than with macramé feathers and leaves. You may need the following materials and follow along in the video below to learn how to create those feathers. Go ahead, and do it.

Requirements

- 4 mm Single Cotton Cord
- Inexorable steel Comb
- Measuring Team
- Cord Lengths:
- Feather # 1 (Width 11 cm, Height 14 cm)
- 1 x 40 cm Edge
- 14 x (13–15 cm)

Feather # 2 (length 11 cm, height 14 cm)

- 1 x 90 cm Strand
- Strand 1 x 150 cm
- Strand 14 x (13-15 cm)

Feather # 3 (Width 11 cm, Height 14 cm)

- 1 x 30 cm Edge
- 1 x 80 cm Layer
- Strand 8 x (13-15 cm)

Macramé Mason jar Plant Hanger

After you have done a few tiny macramé tasks, now is the time to change the knob gradually on your macramé abilities. This tutorial is a perfect segway into learning how to create a macramé of a medium scale.

Macramé Mason jar hangers are nearly similar to a macramé plant hanger and are designed to display smaller home decorations such as candles, cacti, chocolate, and many other kinds of smaller items. This concept for a macramé project is perfect for someone who wants to develop their macramé abilities, which does need more rope than the typical macramé projects. You will look at around 1 – 2 hours to complete this mission, and use six forms of knots. – Larynx head knot, berry knot, double half-hitch knot, square knot, knot picking.

When you begin to venture into medium / larger macramé designs, it is important to consider how many cords and lengths you need for the project. A thumb rule is to follow is to subtract the total duration of the job by 4 to get the duration of the cord in which you intend to operate. When you split the rope in half and tie it to a dowel/ring utilizing the head knot of a lark, you will still need to subtract the amount by two too.

Requirements:

- Long Cotton Beach Cord
- A large metal ring or wooden ring
- Scarves
- Measuring Team

Cord Length:

- 6 x 22 cm
- 1 x 22 cm

3.2 Macramé Table Runner

All you need to learn is three easy knots, and you have a charm layer that works at every season. When you are acquainted with the knots shared here, you can tailor your own table runner to suit your specific table duration, or alter it entirely and build a hanging macramé wall.

Supplies:

- 12″ Holden Multiple
- 22 strands of 16 "cotton rope loops measuring 3 mm
- Hooks over the entrance
- 2m of cotton dowel hanger twine
- Scissors

1. Attach cotton twine to either end of your dowel or hang it from your hooks above the entrance. Fold in half the first 16′ rope loop, and build the head knot of a lark over the dowel.

2. Keep applying the head knot of a lark to each 16′ string of rope until you have 22 overall. That will send you 44 functioning strands.

3. Move the outer right rope over the top of all the other ropes (to the left) and drape the end to the hook at your entrance. This will be the basis for the next row of knots called a half hitch, which creates a horizontal row—Utilizing the second rope to attach a single knot across the cord that you've already stretched over so that it's around 6″ below the dowel.

4. Form a second knot over the base strand utilizing the same thread. It is considered a knot semi-hitch.

5. Make sure they are clear and correct.

6. Continue from outside for the second, third, and fourth rope and make another half-hitch knot, so it's tight and so on. You are going to start looking at trends. It is a Half-Hitch lateral.

7. Keep linking successive knots all the way around in one knot. You do not want this to be so close that the space at the edges is drawn back.

8. Utilizing the outer four strands from the right again, and build a square knot around 1.5" below the horizontal knots rows.

9. Avoid the next four strands (five through eight) and Utilizing strands nine through 12 to form another square knot. Continue to skip four, join four before you get through all the way.

10. Beginning right again, Utilizing the four strands you have missed (five through eight) and tie a square knot below the dowel around 3".

11. Keep binding four-strand missed sets in square knots until you complete the sequence.

12. Take the two outer strands out to the hand at the top. In phase seven, Utilizing strands three to six to build another square knot about 11" below the horizontal row of knots. In addition, use the next four strands to construct another square knot over the last square knot, around 1.5".

13. Go all the way around, as shown. With the last two lines, you will not achieve something.

14. Follow measures three through seven to build another series of horizontal half-hitch knots beginning from the right side again.

15. Utilizing the same base strand of rope beginning from the left side and build another horizontal half-hitch row of knots around 2.5″ below the previous. In this one, you are going to be operating from left to right.

16. Beginning on the left hand, build a row of square knots without missing any strands below the horizontal line of knots, around 1″ away. Instead, construct a second row of square knots by missing the first two threads on the left before joining a complete row of square knots together. It is regarded as an alternating square knot. You do not want a lot of room between those rows, and you can draw them together closely as each square knot is applied.

17. Repeat until you have a minimum of about 13 rows of alternating square knots. This portion is the core of your table runner, and anything else from this stage should echo what you have already woven above.

18. Attach another half-hitch horizontal row of knots beginning from the outer left side and making your way to the center.

19. Utilizing the same base rope to travel Bottom around 2.5″ to create another horizontal half-hitch series of knots that travel from right to left.

20. Skip the outer two rope strands to the right for this segment, and then make a square knot Utilizing strands three to six. Skip strands from seven to ten, and use strands from 11 to 14 to tie

another square knot. Repeat, so for every four strands, you missed. Across the left-hand side, you should find six lines.

21. Skip one and two sections on the left side and bind three to six strands into a square knot approximately 1.5″ below the last set of square knots. Then miss the next four strands and finish the template for the square knots second section. It would put you on the correct side, with six additional threads.

22. Measure 11″ from the last row of horizontal ties and create a square knot utilizing the right side of the outer four lines. Then bind the next four into a square knot over the last knot, around 1.5″.

23. Repeat straight.

Coaster Macramé

Quest for DIY home decor to attach to your living room? Seek to make this cool little coaster with macramé.

To those wanting to get going with their first few macramé creations, Macramé coasters are a perfect novice DIY project. This project should fulfill two roles for you:

1. Help to promote imagination inside yourself
2. It is comfortable and can be used.

This is a perfect idea for a macramé venture if you want to create it relatively simple. It is ideal for those who are trying to get involved with macramé or those who only want to make those coasters with macramé.

Just a heads up, if you are going to build this coaster, be mindful that when it comes to binding and knotting in a circle form, it can get a little complicated. If operating in a circle form, you can note that you are always forced to continually turn around and push the product around the building as you tie. Occasionally it may get a little complicated, but with enough practice, you will be able to ride effortlessly by creating these coasters in no time. You would just need to learn 2 knots for this project: the head knot of the lark and the double half-hitch knot. The prediction time is projected to be 1 hour.

Supplies Needed

- 4 mm Single Cotton Cord
- Hook on crochet

Cord lengths:

- x 52 cm
- 1 x 50 cm Cover

3.3 Macramé Bohemian Style Chairs

Unlike other macramé furniture, you can find online, this Bohemian Style macramé chair one has a large "pocket," so all the tension can be nestled in and swung free. The seat duration is around 40 inches long and 32 inches broad, although extra cords may be expanded in width cutting. Making sure you wind up with a number close (36, 38, 40, etc.).

Requirements

- 6 mm material with rope (322 yards)
- Two 3-inch (heavy-duty) welded metal rings
- Flexible banding
- Optional: 36-inch wooden Dowel with the 3/4-inch thickness (+ dowel cap)

Knots used

- Dual Third Coup (DHH)
- Wrapped Knot
- Alternating Nodes in Square (ASK)
- Barrel bare
- Larks Tie Roof
- Overhand Knot

Cut the cords much like this:

- Upper side supports – 16 cables, 3 yards long each
- Lower side supports -16 cables, each of which is at least 4 yards long
- Seat — 32 strings, each 6.5 yards wide
- Wrapped ties — 2 strings, 36 cm long each

Side Supports

1. Walkthrough one of the rings 8 with 4-yard strings, and align the ends.
2. Put eight of the 3-yard cords on top and bottom.
3. Pull the cord bundle over the underside of the loop.

Tie a Wrapped Knot around the strings, utilizing the following instructions:

1. Guard one end of a 36-inch chord next to the ring to the right of the folded cords. Push 2 inches and fold. Pull the end up again, around the triangle.
2. Tie the edge of the strings, and the one you are utilizing attached at the top.
3. Firmly tie, outward, into the fold.
4. Move the end through the folded field, which appears like a circle, when the knot is 2 inches deep,
5. Push into the safe end at the peak of the tie. It pulls the other end through the Wrapped Tie, as well as the chain. Apply adhesive to the entire knot and cut any extra content from the short cord

Upper Seat Edge

1. Lock or otherwise tie the rings onto the work surface.

2. Take two of the shorter cords from the right chain and two more from the left.

3. This can serve as holding cords to the Hammock Chair's upper side.

4. Roll Bottom from the bottom of the Wrapped Knot 36 to 40 centimeters, depending on how far you like the top of the seat to sit.

5. The four cords will be placed diagonally against each other, and at this stage, they join.

6. List the left cords mentally as one and two, and the right one as three and four.

7. Utilizing them to form a clenched Square Knot. The active strings are one to four, while the fillers are two or three.

Establishing a Seat

1. Push the ends of the four cords in such a way that two go right, while the other two go left, instead of making them dangle.

2. The Hammock Chair seat cables are placed onto the four wires.

3. Fold in half a 6.5-yard cable, and then lay it on top of the four holding cords to the left of the Square knot.

4. Carry the ends across to the back of the four strings, and draw them towards you into the rope that develops. It is a knot of the Larks Head in reverse.

5. Leave some space, for the next move, between this knot and the Square knot.

6. Tie a Half Hitch with the Square Knot end nearest to:

7. Travel over the front edge, then under the cords around. Place it over the cord for which you operate, when you draw it Bottomward.

8. Utilizing the other end to even create a Half Hop. Strengthen ties strongly.

9. Move the first knot to the right, so that it lies on the Square Knot.

10. Perform step 5 with 6.5-yard cords left. The middle of the Hammock Chair will have 16 cables placed to either side of the SK.

11. Stage 6: Tie the 6.5-yard cords to the first row of Alternating Square Knots (ASK). Begin with cord one and travel all the way to cord 64, joining the knots in a horizontal line.

12. They will stop just below the above mounting knots. Utilizing four cords (2 fillers) per knot, Hold the ties tightly tied and secure as soon as possible.

13. Phase 7: Attach further ASK rows, and there is 1-inch of room between the rows.

14. The numbered rows also continue with cord three and end with cord 62. The numbered ODD rows start on cord one and end on cord 64 (same as row1).

15. Start by counting the shorter strings, until you have only 10 inches of material remaining.

Lower Seat Bottom

If you have not already done so, place the Hammock Chair by the bands.

1. Choose two of the longest cords from the right triangle, and another two from the left. Diagonally transfer all four of these strings, against each other. Measure 60 inches from the Enclosed Knot Bottomward. That is the reason the cords are meant to join.

2. Position the bottom of the seat near these holding cords before going on to the next stage, to test the depth of the Hammock Chair.

3. The lower seat section needs to shape a deep pocket, as seen in the picture at the top of the list. When you like the bottom edge to rise out further, you will see the gap between the Wrapped Knot and the spot where the cords touch. Do not put in too many, or the place is not going to be comfortable.

4. Phase 9: After the proper positioning of these lower holding strings, tie a tight Square Knot to connect them together. This is similar to what you did in stage 3.

5. Phase 10: Push the ends of the current holding cords in such a way that two go right, while the other two go left, instead of making them dangle. Utilizing Double Half Hitches to tie half of the cords from seat to the right of the Square Knot, and the same to the left.

6. Add glue to the entire DHH row and require drying before starting.

7. Tie a Barrel Knot for each thread, resting under the Hammock Chair arm, at the bottom edge.

Finish The Seat By Selecting One Option:

- Tie the ends into seat spaces. Next, you should shorten them a little then make sure that they are at least 2 inches thick. Keep the ends in place Utilizing adhesive.
- Cut the strings, and then leave the fringe, so that they stick on.

Side Supports

1. Organize the remaining cords into sets of two, for the right side help.
2. You must travel from the bottom up to the top of the Hammock Chair while you add them to the seat configuration on the right side. Look at the seat and note that within the rows of Square Knots, there are wide gaps around the bottom.
3. Slide from the top into a gap at the end of one of the side help cords. Repeat the same for the second chord, putting it near the first chord but in another room.
4. Be sure that the part that emerges from the ring is clear, despite some friction.
5. Knead the ends into an Overhand tie. Drive it as far as possible.
6. Tie another Knot Overhand next to the previous one.
7. Make sure it sits in the back of the Hammock chair style, after tightening it up.

8. Bring the ends to the front of the seat before continuing to the next stage.

9. Replicate step 11 to the right for the remaining side supports. Always utilizing the longer cables, as the bottom half of the seat will be protected. Make sure they are lined out equally. They use the shorter cords when you step up to the tip.

10. Repeat measures 11 and 12, supporting supports on the left leg. Attempt to position them on the right side, along the same sides. Make changes as required to the ties so that the Hammock Chair hangs equally, before going on to the next move.

11. Go back to where you began, and move through another gap at the ends of the side supports, farther in (to the left). Then again, bind the ends together, as in step 11, with two Overhand ties.

12. Apply so to all the other aids on both the left and the right sides. When completed, add the glue to the knots and allow the knots to heal before starting.

13. The residual material may be used for creating a fringe from the side supports. You may even finish them off by adding additional knots to the bench. Another choice is to attach Barrel knots in each, so they remain true to the ties of the Square. Break off the excess stuff and add adhesive.

14. Phase 16: Utilizing chain or strong rope to tie the hammock chair to a branch or powerful loop that passes through the rings.

Simple add-on to a Dowel

It is optional to use a dowel, so it stabilizes the chair and helps it feel sturdier.

1. Drill chain or rope holes at either end to move through. Slide the rings onto the Dowel, and then position them above the holes.

2. Utilizing leftover cord bits to loop many times around the rings and Dowel, to keep them in place.

3. You should bundle them and bind the two ends together with a Barrel Knot when you are done.

4. Ensure sure the ties are as secure and add glue as necessary. Attach caps with Dowel at either hand.

3.4 Macramé Chandelier

Depending upon the availability of your resources, you can make anything from a lampshade, nursery decor, or bohemian ceiling hanger for your room. You are only limited to your imagination. Below mentioned is how you can make a chic macramé chandelier for your room or hallway.

Requirements

- Lampshade
- Scissors
- 35m Of Cotton Rope
- Iron

How to Create

1. Get 35 meters of 0.5 cm of cotton three-strand rope (40 yards of 3/8 inch cord) for this job, and split into three strands for a more comfortable feel. Therefore, this will give you 105 m of rope (114 yards 3/8-rope). Whether you do not want three-strand rope or choose to undo it, select 105 m instead of the 35 m. You will end up with a macramé chandelier with a length of 25 cm for the macramé portion and a range of 20 cm for the tassel component (10 inches for the macramé and 8 inches for the tassel).

2. For the foundation, deconstruct a cheap lampshade measuring 30 cm (12) "in diameter. You want the wrapping covered so that the wire is left over.

3. Cut the rope to fit first, then unwrap it into three coils. The calculation for figuring out the string's duration is the length of the final woven chandelier times 6, as you will divide the pieces in half before knotting them to the base of the lampshade.

4. Unravel the rope and then iron it to make it straighter to get the beautiful soft tassel to feel.

5. Fold the two pieces of rope in half before connecting them with a reverse larks head knot to the base of the lampshade, as seen below.

6. Start on the chandelier with the first row by tying half knots.

7. Measure one "from the top row of knots, and continue knotting the first row of knots.

8. Measure one "Bottom again after completing the first row and continue knotting the second row of square knots utilizing alternating strands from the previous row.

9. The next row would be two half knots rows with no gap between them, which produces a dense woven border at the bottom.

10. Suppose we do some twisting half knots. There's no way to do this because the knots will start turning on their own if you begin knotting. We have created 15 half knots on each one, and we have ended up with 4' long twisted bits.

11. Measure the twisted parts, and change them, so the lengths are the same, then we'll add two more rows of half knots at the bottom to create a dense border.

12. Feels like what the chandelier's underside after the underside border is knit.

13. The final step is to calculate the perfect tassel length and snip away the excess cord.

3.5 Macramé Shelving

A macramé shelf is a beautiful place to position things such as books, herbs, and candles in the house. Adjust the color of the yarn or the style of the knot for a shelf idea that appeals to your specific taste. Simple to transfer, and easy to create, a macramé shelf is a perfect way to update a room's decor easily.

Requirements

- Circle 2-inch diameter macramé shelf with double hand-hold cutouts
- Yellow cotton yarn
- Clippers

How to Create

1. Place 2 feet diameter on a flat surface with a triangular macramé shelf and double handhold cutouts.
2. Cut two yellow thread bits lengthwise to eight cm. Fold the yarn in half and cut each section in the middle to make four separate pieces of yarn.
3. Lay the four-thread threads out lengthwise, and ensure that the sides are uniformly lined up.
4. Drag the ends of the yarn through the handhold cutouts at the bottom corner of the rack.
5. Pull 6 inches of the yarn ends in half to build a loop and draw the remaining yarn ends to construct a knot through the thread. Pull to grip harder.
6. Utilizing the two middle strands of yellow yarn as a foundation, place the strand in a backward L-shape from the right side of the community across the top of the band.

7. Thread the strand below the two center strands from the left side going up and between the reverse L-shape and the farthest strand on the top. To build a beautiful macramé knot, tap tightly.

8. Repeat the cycle to build a second knot, immediately below the first knot. Move the first knot up to reach the second.

9. Continue to design macramé knots until six are in rows.

10. 1Utilizing four additional yellow yarn strands to replicate the cycle on top of the same cutout with the same hand lock.

11. Assemble the excess yarn at the ends of both knotted macramé strings and thread into one knot.

12. Replicate the entire process on the other side of the circular shelf for handholding cutout.

13. Hold the shelf on either side from the two top knots, so the shelf is parallel to the table.

14. Put a vine, paper, or candle onto the show macramé table.

Chapter 4:
Macramé for Your Garden

Thanks to a fascination with all things that involve craft and imagination, the 70s obsession for knotting anything from designer bags to window boxes in twine or ropes has made a comeback. Macramé provides a gloss layer to the interiors and they are often a fascinating way to incorporate greenery. With only the involvement of two ties, you could create a basic macramé. Here are a number of beginner projects for your garden.

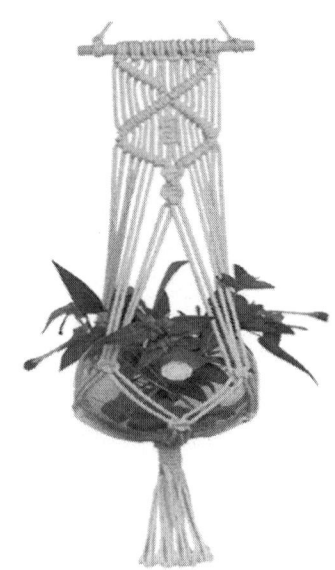

4.1 Basic Garden Décor Utilizing Macramé

Here is a convenient and straightforward little project on the patio to dress up your flowerpot range. Why not offer them a touch of extra flair for the pots with these sweet little macramé collars?

Decorated Flower Pot

This design with Macramé is a perfect way to style a ceramic plant pot for the balcony, or even inside your house.

Requirements

- Glue / Adhesive
- A Terra Cotta 6 1/2 "flower bowl and pot saucer
- 7 1/3 yards 5 ply natural jute rope, scale # 72
- 4 Wooden circular beads, either 12 mm or 16 mm

How to Create

1. Break the project filler string to 1 1/3 yards.
2. Split the project knotting string to 6 yards.
3. Pin the filler string from one end of the Macramé board approx. 12 inches.
4. Pull the knotting cord in half, and then place the cord core on the Macramé board under the filler cable.
5. Attach a pin-side Square Tie. Utilizing two cords knotting around the filler cable core.

6. Attach a string of Sonnets Square Knot, which will then match securely around the rim of the flowerpot. The Sinnet's duration must depend upon the pot's exact diameter. Measure sometimes.

7. Position the Sinnet into the clay pot and glue bottom.

8. Tie the strings of 2 fillers tightly together.

9. Bind these filler cords (now one thread) to the top knotting thread such that all four cords from the Sinnet hang Bottom.

10. Put a bead, at varying lengths, on each thread.

11. To keep the bead stable, tie or attach an Overhand Knot below each bead.

12. Place yet another bead at various lengths on each chain.

13. Place each bead under another Overhand Tie.

14. Trim and bind-knot to hold the ends fused

4.2 Macramé Multi-Plant Hanger

You can create a plant hanger with macramé in several styles. Many instructions are much more difficult and time-consuming to execute, however. These macramé plant hanger patterns for newcomers are a great starting point if you want to create anything simple and convenient.

Such DIY macramé plant hangers come in a number of sizes and types, and with little or no practice, each design is easy enough to complete. There are also several creative embellishments that render your macramé project appear customer and more polished.

It is nice to practice some simple macramé knots on some unused rope parts first before you make a plant hanger. Understanding the ties can make macramé directions far simpler to grasp.

How to Build a Plant Hanger with Macramé

1. Bring all eight pieces of cord together, split in half, and loop around the pipe.

2. Utilizing your 5-foot long string piece, tie a knot in a loop right under the band.

3. Take four strands and tie one knot in a square. Repeat six times.

4. Repeat this pattern for the next 4-cord group, repeat with the residual cords.

5. Leave a distance of two 1⁄2 centimeters, and make a knot of half-square.

6. Repeat until a 5-inch spiral has been formed.

7. Follow the sequence with the remaining groups of knots.

8. Leave a 6-inch distance to build a square crossover knot Utilizing the first group's two right cords, and the neighboring group's two left cords.

9. Repeat with classes left in the knot.

10. Leave a 6-inch gap and build another square knot crossover by reversing the cords from the previous stage.

11. Leave a distance of three 1/2 inches and make a knot at the circle.

12. Trim extra cord to produce a finish on the tassel.

Ways to decorate your Plant hanger with Macramé

Now that you have developed your simple plant hanger for macramé, here are two innovative ways you can carve them up and render them your own.

Dip-Dyed plant hanger in Macramé

Dip dying is a simple way to give your macramé plant hanger a splash of color. Note, the further you dip it in the reaction mixture, the deeper the hue.

1. You can soak-dye your macramé plant hanger in 5 simple measures here:

2. Arrange dye solution as indicated by the box. Assure that you are Utilizing a glass container or cup to avoid staining.

3. Gently tap the hanger until 1/3 of the circumference is immersed into the water.

4. Thread over a wooden dowel, the upper part of the plant hanger, and position over the container or bowl gap. It should leave the

hanger hanging while the bottom portion is painted. Hang on for 30 minutes.

5. Take the hanger from the solvent for the dyeing. Rinse out the residual pigment in the warm spray. Ring Bottom, before pure water runs.

6. Let dry absolutely.

Embroidered plant hanger with Macramé

Another imaginative way to dress things up is to tie the embroidery floss across your macramé plant hanger. Build your own unique designs with different patterns and colors.

Addition of Colorful Bands

1. Lay Bottom a bit of embroidery, and then fold around it. Continue until protected by target duration.

2. To finish the part, use a wooden stick or toothpick to split the floss and tuck in the loose part into the wrapped component.

3. To conclude the sequence, replicate this with certain colors.

Macramé Swing

Life with a fishnet hammock is delightful when you find locations to put it inside as well as outside. Therefore, you can enjoy your days floating over the constant debris of the day, beneath large shade trees and your evenings. Even a sling bed is super-great in a tiny apartment or single room since under the hammock, there is too much free floor space for holding things or an additional sleeping place for a mate. Here is how you can create a fun, easy Hammock utilizing Macramé.

Hammock Utilizing Macramé

The simplest of materials may be made of a Macramé hammock: two poles for the ends, cord for the center and two eyebolts, or any spare rope to cover the completed artwork.

Requirements

- Two 5 ft. long poles (2 ft. wider than you would imagine being the width of completed fishnet bed): two 1/2-3 inches in diameter, fairly wide, flat and sturdy enough to support the weight that will rest in the hammock. You may use tree branches for the ends, or buy wooden or metal poles.

- Hemp cord or any other strong, solid, slip-proof rope, which will stay bound when, tangled. Amount: Six rolls/1310 yards of cord/rope for hammock – do not think about precise proportions, because you should have surplus footage on the ends when finished, (you may opt to include this surplus braid in sturdy bed hanging ropes).

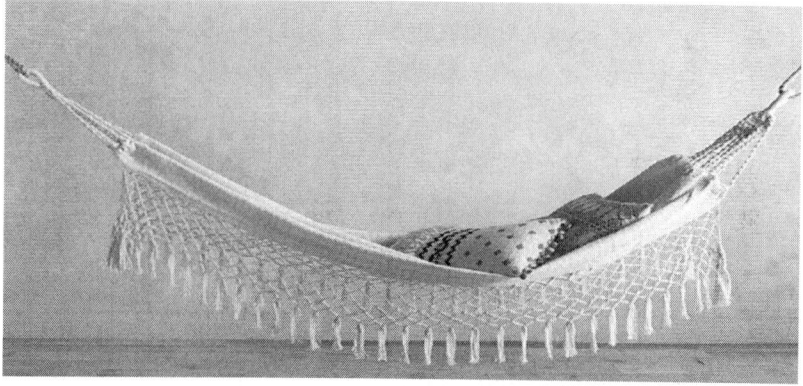

How to Create

1. Start your hammock by swinging flat against a wall on one of the two poles or roots, just above eye level and close to the surface. If two eyebolts are securely fixed in the wall, and two ropes connected to its ends and glued to the bolts, at this stage, attach the pole the starting hammock may imitate a trapeze.

2. If the completed sling bed is permanently hanging as you made it, it's an excellent opportunity right now to check the power of string, ties, and bolts. Do something you can feel to ensure sure the pole is not falling, and the hooks are not slipping out of the ground.

3. Now split the rope into 40 sections of 32 yards each for the hammock squad. Fasten each rope — at its midpoint — to the pole by doubling the strand and taking the thread under the branch and back to the front where the cord 's long ends can be pulled through the circle. Firm the first doubled string.

4. At this stage (with just one cord looped across the stick), you might still have an idea of how amazingly simple it will be to hopelessly tangle 80 individual tails (each 32 yards long.) in order to take care of this issue until it has any possibility of forming.

5. Coil single long tail into a sleek, lightweight bobbin. Start by twirling the first string back and forwards one hand's thumb and little finger until all you have left is one yard or so of twine. In addition, tie up the bobbin with the yard-long open edge — so it will not break apart.

6. Undo the bobbin-making cycle for the second string from the first loop and add all the other strings to branch one by one and shorten them into double bobbins you are heading along with.

7. You will finish this first move in having your hammock equally spread around the center three feet of your five-foot-long pole with 40 double loops (80 different strings and bobbins) at both edges of the line, the foot or two of "clean" room is your

promise that neither of the cords would fall off the staff. You are able to tie.

8. The simplest and best tie for your hammock is the same plain old strong square knot you created your entire life. Except that each one you tie on this project will have two "extra" cords running through the middle of it.

9. Let us begin with the initial four strings on the left end of the pole (the first two double loops). Separate outer two cables from the inner two.

10. Pull the gray cord to the right, and put two white strings over the center. Then pass the black twine over the portion of the gray cord on the left side of the two middle cords, under the center white lines, then on the right side over the grayline. Now, hold the two middle strings straight, draw the gray and black cords into a knot that is tight. You're half done.

11. Wrap up the square knot by taking the first move in the opposite direction. Take the black twine (which is now to the center-right) and pass it under the two white middle lines, going back south. Then loop the gray rope under the black twine (still on the left), over the two white strings and beneath the black twine (going against the wall) on the center. Draw both the gray and black cords tightly up while you keep the two white strings straight until the first square knot is complete. Now tie the same knot around the branch all the way across each team of four cords.

12. The second row of knots is connected in the same way, other than that the ties in the first row are spaced to break between

them. Nothing to it: just miss the first two strings as you commence Row No. 2, and then create the first knot with the next four cords. The left-hand string will be the old center-right chord in either knot in the second section, the two center cords will be old gray and black strings, and the right-hand rope will be a middle-left rope from the above section. Forget regarding the two strings "untied" at each end of Row 2. Let them hang in the third row of knots and bring them in.

13. If the limb or pole is marginally crooked, the same minor irregularity will extend to each row of knots before you spread the hammock directly Bottom.

14. The hammock remaining will be a whiz. Only try to keep steady with the ties.

15. Pull an additional piece of cord through the hammock, and attach the ends and center to the branch to get your working area back to a reasonable point.

16. Create the sling bed from five to 7 feet in either position (depends entirely on how tall you are). The hammock can extend, so do not lengthwise go crazy, or you will find yourself touching your toes as your rear bounces the wall.

17. If, when you finish off the bunk, you consider the completely last row of knots irregular, or the hammock end of the square, twist by twist.

18. Attaching The Secondary Pole With A Double Half Hitch - When your hammock is as big as you like, you'll finish the bed by wrapping all 80 cords across the second limb (after you've checked the first pole for strength).

19. To make this task a third row of knots up from the base of the hammock and attach the cross cord at many points to the top branch such that the last row of knots hangs flat at a convenient working position.

20. Now the bottom pole is lying parallel to the last series of knots, and you can macramé it to the hammock. Attach this point to the top crosspiece with additional rope such that the second worker is parallel to the surface, balanced and near enough to the last row of knots such that as you pull on the cords, those knots can almost touch the second pole.

21. You must use another tie, named the double half hitch, to grip the hammock's macramé body to the second pole. Start this procedure as described above by placing the workers over all the cords. Then put the first chord up from below, across the pole and back Bottom the other right side of the chord's main leg. Next, pull the twine up from below and second time around the handle. In addition, bring it to the left of the main cord on this pass, and thread it Bottom through the loop that you just pulled through. Pull the cord's key component high, and then tighten it Bottom, the half-hitch end.

22. Attach an equal half hitch to the next rope and start to work the way left until you have knotted each twine to the second staff, and both ends of the string are equally hanging from the spike.

23. At this stage, extending the hammock to our securely to test for "line" and uniformly spaced tautness is a good idea. When you are happy that the final product is as perfect as you can get it,

you can tie the bed cords finally to the second pole, and there is almost no risk they will operate loose.

24. This final structure is achieved with the aid of a square knot. On the bottom, grab the first four cords and make two or three square knots, one right after another. Then tie in the next two or three square ties, four cords and start, knotting four cords at a time, before you meet the end of the string lines.

25. Take off the strings, as big as you like. A suggested length of around two feet separated the strings into five classes and bound with a big overhand knot increasing part. Around one foot of extra twine wisely hangs out of the set.

26. Hovering The Hammock - You can hold your sling bed from the above-described eyebolts, hammer anything out with ropes and trees or hang from ceiling beams on the large fish net sofa. Anyway, create more pressure in advance than you would ever want the bed to bear. This hammock is spacious for one person, and if you all coil around one another, it can fit two or more. Just be sure that your latest piece of aerial furniture is tightly fastened enough to carry you, your mates, and any extra tension and pressure that may be called in to deal.

27. Put a vibrant Egyptian rug or a heavy-pile blanket over your hammock or hang jewels on it for a final touch (wax or glue the rope tips, twist the ends small enough to loop through the accessories and let the twine cool completely). An atmospheric cushion over the ties provides warmth, and you can float hanging lamps, potted plants, cell phones, toys or candy bowls

over your outdoor bed for pure fun pleasure while you spread out.

4.3 Macramé Garden Chairs

Interested in making a personalized macramé lawn chair? Decide on the paint and give a special touch to your own lawn chair by retrofitting an old chair with this DIY macramé lawn chair. Don't throw away those rusty folding lawn chairs, reweave the cover with a brightly colored art string and carry them back to life.

- 200 yards with a 6 mm macramé string
- Crochet Hooks 19.00 mm
- Metal lawn chair frame
- Scissors
- Lighter
- Design

1. Extract webbing or lining from the chair use scissors. Clean out the case.

2. You will want to put your cord roll on the floor within the chair frame to start your rig. It is the cord is simplest positioning over the entire weaving cycle. Create a double square knot beginning on the seat bottom ring, leaving around 6″ of slack at the top. Bear in mind that you can just thread on the straight sections of the frame of your chair, leaving the rounded edges empty.

3. Now pick up your chain, below the center bar and up over the frame end. Then, thread the rope around the chair frame and draw it outwards. Move the crochet hook into the loop you have just created. Push the rope firmly, ensuring that the thread does not come free. Often, to ensure you can bring the hook in the next time around; make sure that the loop lies on the fattest portion of the line. Trust me, when you proceed, this will make your life a lot simpler.

4. Put the chord back Bottom, underneath the center plate, and then over the seat frame top. Wrap the rope around the frame and slide it under the first pair of cords to the edge. Push the crochet hook into the loop much as you did before, letting it lie on the flat portion of the thread. Tightly grab the loose thread, and proceed.

Aluminum Chair Recreation Utilizing Macramé

If you do not want to create a new macramé chair for your garden, you can also try creating an old aluminum one.

Requirements

- A chair in aluminum
- Paracord and macramé cord in various colors but identical in scale (150'-200' overall, depending on the height of the chair)
- Scissors
- Screwdriver on smooth top
- Rubber band

How to Create

1. Pull webbing from your chair by removing the ties and unwinding the posts on the back of your frame afterward.
2. Determine which color you want to continue with, and tie a double knot at the edge of the flat front around your frame cover—leaving only 5″ of hair.
3. Cover the cord at the turn of the chair under the central bar, then up and over the base. Instead, curl back under the curve of the chair, and then coil around the seat frame's bottom edge next to where you began.
4. Both the rows will cover the edges of the picture from the front and over the back. Try to switch colors, or run out of thread. Add a double knot to either the top or bottom edge of the picture, depending on where you end up and make sure you have ample enough cord to tuck in when you are finished. As seen below, you may clip into the next color or cord string too.

5. Weave before the other end of the flat portion of the frame is past you. The rounded corner may have a small negative space, so do not worry. This would be the way it should be.

6. Only attach on the side of the frame with a double knot to continue weaving in the other direction, and leave around 5″ of the tail. Taking your cord under the first four rows and create the triangle shape (two top and two bottoms to get four total), and come up and over with your string. Tuck it under, and you have four more on the other hand. On the other hand, loop the rope around the top of the picture, and head out the same direction you came in as seen above.

7. Wrap around the frame's beginning hand and come up beneath the first four and the next two, and you are missing a minimum of six. Only replicate the same amount on the opposite hand, and then return the way you came in.

8. Keep performing this process of raising two rows if you pass, and then proceed the same path you came from. This will create a pattern that is triangular. Keep working on the chord before you stop or have to add the same color to another hand.

9. For increasing the new triangle, here is what it feels like to shift colors. If you are Utilizing an adult chair, it is recommended that you use a thicker macramé cord to make the job easier.

10. Trim the loose tails to only be long enough to tuck in and relax home. If this was a macramé job, it might be easier to cover the loose ends, but we are just spinning and putting the sophisticated knot tying for another job.

4.4 Macramé Wedding Arch

Ceremony arches are an ideal way to show your unique look. This DIY macramé wedding arch is the right design for an outdoor event, incorporating a friendly touch of bohemia. Macramé provides an atmospheric feel with its knotted technique and allows a perfect background for photographs from ceremonies.

A macramé ceremony arch will bring a unique charm to your wedding while keeping it budgetary efficient and wow your guests, of course.

How to Create

Follow directions on the box to attach all of your backdrop frame's key parts.

1. Spray paint the backdrop Stand's related parts. When clear, finish setting up the frame for the background.
2. Cut the normal cording, so the height of the foreground picture is double that. Fold the cord in two, and then put the two folded over the top handle. Bring the cording ends via the top loop, and pull to lock.
3. Continue stage three before 10 bits of cording have been added, creating twenty bits.
4. Every group of hanging cords has two pieces hanging Bottom. Divide the initial classes into two, and build new two groups. Add these latest classes some two inches deep in knots.
5. Continue to move five until about four vertical rows of knots are joined together.
6. Fall the two center cording parts off your ties for the next round. From hanging these, two items. Once you launch the next round of knots, lower the next row of cording off the knots. Follow this process until you get both sides to the edges of the context.
7. Grab scissors, and then remove the loose cording ends. Starting from the middle cut diagonally, so the cord inside is the shortest and the longest outer cording.
8. Fill a tub with some water and food coloring, and then put the macramé's ends in. Squeeze the macramé and allow it to dry to remove some excess ink.

9. After your macramé has cooled, decorate with fake eucalyptus, the top and side of your ceremony background. Start by wrapping the eucalyptus around the top left of your backdrop, and run them around the pole while you operate. It will hang on to its own, but if not, it should be protected with some floral rope.

10. Enhance the backdrop by adding fake peonies to the top corners of the arch for ceremonies. Feed the peony via the eucalyptus, and then use floral wire to tie it to the background.

Conclusion

When most folks talk about macramé, they imagine hipsters, flower hangers, and have Summer school memories, when they were initially introduced to the knotting technique, also recognized as macramé. "Oh, I remember the macramé," they claim. "I did that when I was little," or, "My mother used to do that." Yeah, there is more to macramé than that — lots more. For many, many years, Macramé has been around here. The practice of knotting emerged first in the Middle East as a way to create nets and decorate the edges of cloth. Seafarers developed this in their voyages, and macramé expanded across the world through flight, commerce and the invasion of distant lands. It had its heyday in the Victorian period, when the art became commonly known. Many of people recall the macramé of the 1970s, but that was far from the onset.

However, today, Macramé's skill and interest means different things to different people; in many respects, the ability is valuable and unique, while for some, it does not matter. Macramé involves tying the loops to stabilize the arms and hands. It can be very relaxing and therapeutic to the body, mind and spirit to make a macramé product; it is also an environmentally friendly art choice.

Those are only two of the advantages of its practitioners that macramé art lovers believe this art form imparts. There are other advantages obtained from macramé, including the numerous decorative objects and valuable goods that macramé produces. Macramé is, by definition, therapeutic. Pulling strings and manipulating them, helps strengthen the hands and arms. It helps loosen down the joints. Many people consider that macramé; an art of repeated knots used to build patterns, is meditative and carries harmony and clarity in mind with it. Some twine and a few simple knots are all a hobbyist needs to discover the immense possibilities provided by macramé. Macramé art requires not a number of materials or equipment. Macramé is making a big comeback. Youth enjoys pattern because it encourages having options available to them to construct beautiful designs that they are eager to use along with show and pals' creativity. They love creating unique pieces, anklets that are like bracelets and bands of solidarity that they could give away as marketplaces or presents.

This book is a complete guide for anyone who wants to learn the skill and creative art of Macramé. Starting from the list of the supplies need to how to utilize them, this book has elaborated everything that a novice would want to.

Printed in Great Britain
by Amazon